Who Has
Your
Heart?

Who Has Your Heart?

The Single Woman's Pursuit of Godliness

Emily E. Ryan

Discovery House Publishers

Books, music, and videos that feed the soul with the Word of God

Box 3566 Grand Rapids, MI 49501

To Jason:
I know God has our hearts,
because in His infinite wisdom,
He decided that they
belong together.

Discovery House Publishers is affiliated with RBC Ministries, Grand Rapids, Michigan.

Discovery House books are distributed to the trade exclusively by Barbour Publishing, Inc., Uhrichsville, Ohio.

Requests for permission to quote from this book should be directed to: Permissions Department, Discovery House Publishers, P.O. Box 3566, Grand Rapids, MI 49501.

Library of Congress Cataloging-in-Publication Data
Ryan, Emily E.
    Who has your heart? : the single woman's pursuit of godliness / Emily E. Ryan.
        p. cm.
    ISBN 1-57293-189-2
    1. Single women—Religious life. I. Title.
    BV4596.S5R93   2006
    248.8'432—dc22   2006025268

Interior design by Nicholas Richardson.

Printed in the United States of America

07 08 09 10 11 / BPI / 10 9 8 7 6 5 4 3 2

Contents

Introduction / 7

PART 1: Unmarried
1. The Urge to Merge / 11
2. The Heroine Search / 27

PART 2: Unnamed
3. Her Gumption / 45
4. Her Genes / 61
5. Her Grace / 77
6. Her Grasp / 91
7. Her God / 109
8. Her Girls / 129
9. Her Grief / 149
10. Her Guarantee / 165
11. Her Guiltlessness / 181
12. Her Guidance / 195

PART 3: Unshakable

13. Before You Shake Your Tambourine / 213
14. The Tambourine Tribute / 225

Introduction

As a single woman, I was in the middle of writing this book when I agreed to go on a blind date with a man named Jason. He was a musician; I was a writer. At the very least, I hoped we would possibly connect on an artistic level.

The date went well, and over dessert he asked me if I was working on any particular writing project. I spent the rest of the evening telling him about Jephthah's daughter and how God had used her story to recapture my heart and change my outlook on being single. He didn't say much as I rambled on for over an hour. He just politely smiled and nodded.

In the days to come, Jason and I discovered that we had connected on far more than an artistic level and, in time, we got married. Most brides thankfully turn their backs on their former lives as singles and embrace their newfound marital status. However, even as a new wife, I found myself retreating into my notes and research on being single. I still had a desire to read books for singles. I still wanted to discuss dating and waiting with my single friends. But more than anything, I could not pull myself away from the message of Jephthah's daughter and my desire to share her story with others.

So in spite of my love for my new husband and the joy I was experiencing as his wife, there was one part of my single life I was not ready to give up yet. I couldn't let go of Jephthah's daughter or the message God gave me through her story, and I wanted to keep writing my book for single women.

I tell you this so that you will not be confused as you read this book. Even though I am now married, the concept of this book began when I, as a single woman desiring a husband, found comfort and hope in the story of Jephthah's daughter, a young woman who, with grace and godliness, successfully struggled through the same challenges I was facing. Her story enabled me, a single woman longing for passion, to realize that complete contentment could only come when my true Bridegroom, Jesus Christ, had my heart.

I hope that He will capture your heart as well as you pursue godliness in this study of Jephthah's daughter. And whether you marry a month from now, a year from now, or never at all, I pray that a piece of your heart will always remember the longing you feel for a groom and the fulfillment you receive from your Bridegroom.

Part One

UNMARRIED

Chapter 1

The Urge to Merge

On the Verge of the Urge

My first "fiancé" was Mr. Rafa, and he was a beautiful man. I met him during evening rehearsals for *The Nutcracker* when I was cast as a Ginger Child and he as the Rat King. Despite his infamous role in the ballet, as long as he wasn't rehearsing in full costume (rat costumes are not attractive), he was mesmerizing to watch. Perhaps it was because he had jet-black hair and blue eyes which, combined with the tights, reminded me of Superman. Or maybe it was that he could dance like Baryshnikov. Whatever it was, when he was at rehearsals, I was the best-behaved six-year-old in the entire cast.

It wasn't long before I decided that I was going to marry Mr. Rafa someday, and I wasn't shy about my decision either. I told everyone: my mom, my dance teachers, and the other Ginger Children. I even told *Mrs.* Rafa (she was not amused). Of course, my naive belief that I would grow older and Mr. Rafa would stay the same age was ill founded, and my first schoolgirl crush ended without incident.

Since then, there have been countless more "fiancés"—men, boys, movie stars, or pizza delivery guys—about whom I've daydreamed and secretly planned our weddings. But Mr. Rafa will always hold a special place in my heart as the first. I admired him from a distance, and looking back I can safely say that he was proof that the Urge to Merge hit me very early in life.

The Urge Emerges

The Urge to Merge hits us all at different times. Some of you are lucky; you didn't get the urge until your thirtieth birthday was circled on the calendar and the celebration invitations were mailed. You didn't think about marriage, much less worry about it, until you noticed an unshakable noise ringing in your ears and realized that it was indeed your biological alarm clock screaming its wake-up call.

Others of you have been pressing snooze on your clock for years. You were the ones who, while in elementary school, bought a red lollipop ring, put it on your ring finger, and (in between licks) paraded it around as an engagement ring. Slowly, you wised up in junior high when you learned that your red candy ring could produce an undesirable (and sticky) result when you ran your fingers through your hair while wearing it. And so you graduated from the sweet fantasy to a more dignified approach to love and life as you played the "What will my future name be?" game. This meant that your book covers in school were transformed into working scratch pads as you practiced writing your first name with the last name of every hunky football player or good-looking track star to ever grace the classrooms of fifth period with his presence. (Though this habit, unlike that of the lollipop ring, some of us never outgrew.)

Submerged in the Urge

It was August 8, 1988—better known as 8/8/88—and I remember it like it was yesterday.

I was only eleven then, and I was vacationing with my family in Wimberley, Texas, at my aunt and uncle's house on the Blanco River. After a long, lazy afternoon of tubing down the river and getting scorched by the summer sun, I dragged my prune-shriveled body to the house and collapsed onto the sofa to revel in the wonders of air conditioning. I closed my eyes and sunk deep into the couch, tuning out the reporters on the evening news and wondering how many close calls I'd had with giant garfish in the river that day (countless, no doubt).

The Urge to Merge hits us all at different times.

After a long commercial break and the last weather forecast of the program, the anchors ended the newscast with an eye-opening human-interest story. Because of the date—8/8/88—the number of weddings performed on that particular Monday outnumbered even the average for weekend weddings. It seemed many couples had chosen that special calendar-friendly date for their weddings in order to make them more memorable.

I scooted to the edge of the sofa and leaned forward to get a better look at the images of the couples that flashed across the screen. I thought about how lucky those women were—they were almost guaranteed wonderful presents on their anniversaries simply because, with a date like that, it would be impossible for their husbands to forget it.

The news blurb ended with the anchors explaining that the next time the dates would align so perfectly would be on September 9, 1999. I immediately began calculating. How old would I be then? Would it be possible for me to plan my wedding on that easy-to-remember, sure-to-get-presents date?

My heart sunk, however, when I realized that I would be twenty-two years old! And though I spent the next commercial break considering it, I finally concluded that the possibility of postponing my future wedding for the mere sake of having a memorable anniversary date was simply not worth it. I wouldn't—I couldn't—wait that long to get married! I'd just have to think of some other way to make my wedding date special.

You can probably conclude from the fact that you're reading this book that 9/9/99 came and went without so much as dinner and a movie, much less a proposal or a wedding. As did 01/01/01, 02/02/02, 03/03/03, and many other dates that I longed to circle on my calendar and decorate with doodled hearts and bells in the margin. Instead, these dates were filled with life-changing events like "Get oil changed" or "Pick up dry-cleaning."

When we have a time frame, an agenda, or a particular date in mind, the urge seems to get stronger, doesn't it? The pressure increases and the drumming of our fingers grows louder and louder as we watch impatiently as our ideal date or perfect bridal age comes and goes without a hint of white to cover our darkened desires.

Maybe you have made similar wishes as you thumbed through

the pages of your leather-bound planner or clicked the stylus of your PDA, inputting everyone's special events but your own. Weddings. Lingerie showers. Housewarming parties. Bachelorette parties. Rehearsal dinners. And the ever-so-dreaded, why-are-you-doing-this-to-me event: the couples shower. If the urge has hit you, any of these events, along with a myriad of others, can trigger you to set yet another hopeful but meaningless deadline as you long for your day in the limelight to begin.

Then again, some of you didn't have to set fake deadlines, because there was once a time when you *did* have your wedding date circled on a calendar. The church was booked. The dress was beautiful. And weekly manicures became a must to highlight the huge rock that sparkled from your left hand.

However, a few months, many fights, and one broken engagement later, you found yourself right back where you started. Your calendar looked like a tic-tac-toe game, as the circle on what would have been your wedding date became an *X* instead. Your beautiful dress went to the back of the closet as you prayed it would still be in style by the time you needed it for real, and your now bare and dull ring finger mocked you with its sudden nakedness.

For those of you with a broken engagement in your past, you have a different viewpoint of the unrealized and unmet deadlines. Yours was not one of mere "wishin' and hopin' and thinkin' and prayin'" that could easily be erased and forgotten once it became but a speck in the rearview mirror of life. It was an actual deadline that involved real people and resulted in very real consequences.

But however real or fabricated the deadlines are that come and go with no avail, the disappointment that follows cannot be denied. Unmet deadlines can create panic and can easily lead to another cycle of misplaced hope, the cycle of the If . . .Then statements.

This variation of the deadline response to the suffocating urgency is the manifestation of the hypothetical syllogism. For those of you who never took Philosophy 101, that's the nerd term for the If . . . Then statement. For example: *If* Andy doesn't ask me to dance by the second verse of Richard Marx's "Right Here Waiting," *then* I'm going to go ask Cliff to dance instead. *If* I'm really "sweet sixteen and never been kissed," *then* I'm destined to be an old maid. *If* I don't have a date to my senior prom, *then* I'll never leave my room again.

These grandiose declarations may seem harmless enough when we're still wearing training bras and braces, but they inevitably culminate into establishing a very rocky mindset as single adults. The statements that start off small and silly can evolve into weighty internal fears:

- If I'm not married by the time I'm x, then . . .
- If I don't get my *Mrs.* degree in college, then . . .
- If my father dies before he gets to walk me down the aisle, then . . .
- If I have to wear one more tacky bridesmaid dress, then . . .
- If I end up being a thirty-year-old virgin, then . . .

I'll admit that I was guilty of thinking about every one of these fears plus many others. They crept into my thoughts, set up camp in my mind, and lingered like unwelcome houseguests. During high school and college, it was easier to suppress the fears and disappointments because I could hide behind masks of busyness or prior life commitments. But when the post-college years began to add up like the bridesmaid dresses in my closet, doubt began to creep in. Perhaps I wasn't pretty enough. Maybe I wasn't "marriage material." Maybe God had simply forgotten about me.

The Urge Surges

And then, *it* happened. The ultimate If . . . Then situation came to be. My sister, Meghan—four years younger than I and only nineteen at the time—became engaged. Her first date with Ryan was to the movies, and by the time that same movie was released on video, she was sporting a beautiful new engagement ring and picking out china patterns. A word of advice: Don't ever say, "*If* my little sister gets married before I do, *then* . . ." because not even sugar can sweeten the taste when you have to eat *those* words.

I was shocked. This was definitely not how my life was supposed to work out. I was the older sister. The type A personality. The one who *made* things happen. I was supposed to be the leader in all of life's new ventures and milestones: college, marriage, first homes, babies. She was supposed to learn from *my* successes and failures, not the other way around.

Of course it didn't help that Ryan was perfect for her. He was a Christian, played in the church orchestra, got along with our brothers, and was just finishing up his last year of dental school. I was happy for Meghan. Really, I was. She deserved all of these wonderful blessings plus many others; I just selfishly wanted her to receive those blessings *after* I did.

Needless to say, there's nothing like catching the bouquet at your little sister's wedding to demolish all deadlines and fears and make the Urge to Merge *surge!* I felt like God had forgotten about me. Like the fulfillment of my dreams and desires passed me by and landed on other people. God was raining down marriage blessings like manna, and I was the only one under an umbrella.

Have you experienced an event that caused your urge to surge? Maybe you were casually flipping through the Sunday socials section of your community newspaper when you saw her picture listed under "Engagements": the exasperating girl whose artwork was always chosen for display all through elementary school, stole two of your junior high boyfriends, and then secretly

> God was raining down marriage blessings like manna, and I was the only one under an umbrella.

sabotaged your laboratory experiments in freshman chemistry class. "How can someone love *her* when no one seems to love me?" you ask yourself as you fold the paper and realize that you just found the perfect lining for your pet parakeet's birdcage.

Or maybe you were blindsided by your postman one day when he delivered an unexpected off-white envelope to your mailbox. You threw your bills to the side and ripped into the envelope to find your ex-boyfriend's wedding invitation enclosed. What made it worse was that the inner envelope was addressed to you *and Guest,* reiterating the fact that he had found his lifelong *and Guest,* and you couldn't even muster up a date to his wedding.

The Urge Diverges

For me, it was my sister's wedding—The Year of Meghan—
that made my urge surge. And the more that the urge surged,
the more my faith wandered. Instead of persevering down the
safe and promising road of trust and hope, I casually meandered
onto a path that diverged from the main road. A trail that was
so shaded I could no longer see the Son. A path headed straight
to Bittersville.

I didn't notice my thoughts and attitudes changing during
The Year of Meghan, but in hindsight I can see that they did.
They say that if you're going to cook a frog (not that you're going
to), the best way is to put the frog in cold water and slowly turn
up the heat until it reaches a boil. The frog will not notice the
gradual change in temperature and will allow itself to be boiled
without protest. This is how bitterness works. It doesn't surprise; it creeps. Bitterness is like getting a sunburn on a cloudy
summer day: You don't notice the heat, but you certainly can't
deny your tomato-red skin the next day. "Each heart knows
its own bitterness, and no one else can share its joy" (Proverbs
14:10).

The funny thing is that I actually tried *not* to become bitter. When I heard myself make a snide comment or snap at
someone who asked an innocent question about my love life, I
tried to cover it up or laugh it off. That's when I rediscovered
an old monologue from my college drama days that seemed to
express my innermost thoughts better than I ever could myself.
It's called "Non-Bridaled Passion" and is taken from a musical
revue entitled, "A . . . My Name is *Still* Alice."

In this humorous monologue, a young woman in her thirties approaches a bridal registry consultant of a major department store to register for gifts. The consultant asks the young woman when she is planning to get married, and she explains that she has no fiancé and no wedding date in mind. She is frustrated because she has been buying gifts for all of her friends who are getting married—in her opinion, they are not the only ones who should be receiving gifts. The following monologue ensues in response to the confused objections of the bridal registry consultant.

Woman: This voice inside my head started screaming at me. It said, "Why do you keep buying presents for people who have already found everything they want?" Or words to that effect. I don't remember exactly. I do recall that the voice sounded resentful. And I had to agree with it. I mean, isn't it enough that they were lucky and found each other? That they fell in love and made a commitment? That they'll be splitting the rent and filing jointly? They've found someone who'll give them a *foot massage* whenever they want! They've already won the sweepstakes, why do they get the door prizes too? Why do they get to register for things like . . . like . . . like a cookie jar shaped like a giant eggplant, or a set of "really good knives"? THEY'RE BECOMING A TWO-INCOME FAMILY, WHY CAN'T THEY BUY THEIR OWN KNIVES???!!! Now then. I need things. I am not getting married and I need things. I need better towels. Matching luggage. A pasta machine. And sterling silver candlesticks—put me down for two pair. Come on, just do it! You registered Ann and Deena, Lisa, Jane and Cindy, I *insist* on registering too! . . . I *know* I'm single; I confront that fact every day of my life. It's fine! I accept it! But I'm not *staying* single without the same material goods as my married friends. *My ship is coming in if I have to tow it myself!* . . . Do you really want to know when the happy event is? It's a week from Saturday. I'm throwing a shower for myself, officially announcing a life of singlehood. And the beauty of it is, I won't have to return anything if it doesn't work out!

It was about the time I started thinking that throwing a shower for myself might actually be a *good* idea that I realized I wasn't becoming bitter anymore. I *was* bitter. And wouldn't you know it, bitterness was *not* a pretty color on me. But slowly my eyes adjusted to the darkness around me, and I could see again. *So, this is what bitterness looks like.*

Maybe you're reading this book because you feel yourself becoming bitter too. Perhaps your apartment has become the launching pad for engagements, none of them your own, as roommate after roommate passes through your life on their way to marriage leaving you with nothing but mismatched silverware and a pile of dog-eared bride's magazines laughing at you from your coffee table. Maybe family gatherings have become awkward for you, as suddenly all of your siblings have found love and marriage, leaving you to eat alone at the kiddy table with your nieces and nephews.

It's scary to realize how easily bitterness and discontentment can sneak into our thoughts. But thankfully, bitterness is like the tick of a clock in the silence of the night. Hours may pass with the sound ticking by unnoticed, but the second someone asks you, "Do you hear that noise?" it's suddenly all you hear. Once I realized I was bitter, it was all I could think about.

Purging the Urge

Because of my oldest-child, type A personality, I realized that I had to *do* something. The bitterness had to be conquered, and the urge had to be *purged*. And so I began doing what was natural for me: I read. I read books about being single. Books about preparing for marriage. Books about dating. Books about *not* dating. My library became full of books regarding the single life written from just about every angle possible.

Some of them were really good, but inevitably I'd turn to the back cover to read the "About the Author" section and find the same trend over and over again. *Mrs. So-and-So lives in Such-and-Such Town with her loving husband of twenty-something years. Together they have 2.5 impeccably well-behaved children, an adoring poodle named Fluffy, and a perfectly engineered white picket fence that surrounds their flawless home in the suburbs.*

For some unexplainable reason (probably the bitterness again), once I learned that the sources of these scripturally based opinions were married, I would immediately disregard all of their pearls of wisdom. *Of course they believe all that,* I thought. *They get to greet their husbands every night after work with a hot home-made dinner and an even hotter welcome-home kiss. It's always easy to trust God in hindsight.* (For a note about my own personal marital status, please don't throw this book down without reading the introduction first!)

Then there were the books written by other singles, but again,

I felt like the connection stopped just short of a closed circuit. Either the author presented an, "I am woman, hear me roar," type attitude that made me feel like I was being treacherous to my gender just by desiring a husband, or they presented a Super-Christian, hyperspiritual viewpoint that made me feel like I was neglecting God Himself in my desire to be married. I felt like I was caught somewhere in the middle of the single-life spectrum, and I couldn't seem to find an author that spoke to my *heart*.

The Urge Converges

"Let us fix our eyes on Jesus, the author and perfecter of our faith" (Hebrews 12:2). It's funny how sometimes the most obvious and simple answers are right in front of us, and we don't even realize it. Perhaps it's a blessing that I didn't fully connect with any of the authors I read before. It forced me to turn to *The Author*, which is something I should have done in the very beginning.

It may seem that your longing to have a husband and your desire to trust God's plan are tearing you in two different directions. But find peace in the fact that there *is* one place that those two repelling forces can converge, and that's in the arms of our Father. When I finally turned to Him with all my anger and beat His chest in anguish that my life was not as I had hoped, He didn't stop me from pounding. He simply wrapped His arms around me so tightly that, in time, I finally stopped fighting on my own.

My prayer for you as you read this book is not necessarily that you will connect with me, the author, or that you will agree with everything I have to say. My prayer is simply that this will point you back towards your heavenly Father. This is not a book about dating. It's not about preparing for marriage. And it's definitely not a book about how to be single. For if our search is merely to discover who we are in our marital status, we've missed the ultimate quest, which is discovering who we are *in Christ*.

Together we'll look at a girl in Scripture who can show us who God wants us to be in Him. We won't learn her name, for she remains unnamed. We won't meet her husband, for she is unmarried. But we will study her character, for she is unshakable.

> For if our search is merely to discover who we are in our marital status, we've missed the ultimate quest, which is discovering who we are *in Christ.*

And she's not simply a godly woman who teaches how to be single. Rather she's a single woman who teaches us how to be godly.

The Urge to Merge will not go away, but my prayer is that the source of your attraction will change. Rather than longing to merge with a faceless man known only in your dreams, I pray you'll long to merge with our God and Creator instead.

Your Urge to Merge

1. The Urge to Merge hits us all at different times. Looking back, when would you say the desire to marry first entered your thoughts? Who are some "fiancés" you've had since then, and who was the first?

2. Most of us set arbitrary deadlines for ourselves regarding love and marriage, whether we realize it or not. What are some of your own deadlines and expectations for the ideal time to marry? What makes those time frames ideal?

3. Read the story of Jacob and Rachel in Genesis 29:14–30. In verse 26, what does Laban give as the reason for delaying Jacob's marriage to Rachel? How do current customs and cultural trends affect your own thoughts about marriage?

4. As we go about our everyday lives, there are always factors that seem to trigger the Urge. Of the following triggers, which ones cause your Urge to surge, and which ones do not affect you? What are some triggers of your own that are not on the list?

Holidays	Weddings	Parental Pressures
Loneliness	Sexual Desires	Desire for Children
Birthdays/Age	_____	_____

5. When our self-made deadlines pass us by or when the Urge
   is triggered yet again by one of the factors listed above,
   sometimes shades of bitterness can creep into our thoughts.
   Rate the bitterness level in your own life on a scale of 1 to
   10, with 1 being "I don't even own a map to Bittersville"
   and 10 being "I'm the Mayor of Bittersville," What does
   Ephesians 4:31 say we are to do with bitterness?

6. Read Lamentations 3:19–23. Now focus on verses 22 and
   23 and name at least three truths that we can call to mind
   when bitterness creeps in.

7. This is not a book about a godly woman who teaches us how
   to be single but rather about a single woman who teaches
   us how to be godly. Knowing this, what do you hope to
   gain from reading it?

8. *Memorize* Hebrews 12:2: "Let us fix our eyes on Jesus, the
   author and perfecter of our faith."

Chapter 2

The Heroine Search

The Quest Begins

I don't want to mislead you. Turning to the Author and searching in His Word does not necessarily give us answers overnight. Sure, sometimes it does. And other times you search for years never finding anything, until one day you realize that it was not the destination through which God spoke to you but rather the journey itself.

As I turned to the Bible in my quest to find God's heart in my singleness, I quickly discovered that I needed a role model. A woman to imitate. A lady to admire. A heroine to learn from. This was a quest that most certainly could not be accomplished overnight, for the pages of the Bible are full of godly women who sought the Lord and accomplished great things in His name.

I'd heard all of their stories before. Ruth. Rahab. Mary. Esther. The list was significant but not impossible to explore.

So the Heroine Search began, with a roll call of these famous and oft-cited ladies of faith.

The Proverbs 31 Woman

It never failed. In my search for a heroine, this woman's name was always at the top of everyone's list of recommendations. The spunky Proverbs 31 chick. The woman known for her verbs. For singles, wives, mothers, and grandmothers alike, this gal is the epitome of feminine Christianity. She is the type of lady that every woman longs to become and every man longs to find, and her brief appearance in Proverbs 31:10–31 is one of the most popular passages in the Old Testament.

> As I turned to the Bible in my quest to find God's heart in my singleness, I quickly discovered that I needed a role model.

No doubt she lived up to her reputation when I studied her. This chick manages to accomplish more in her short cameo at the end of this book of wisdom than most women accomplish in a lifetime. In fewer than twenty-five verses, this woman does it all. She brings, she selects, she works, she gets, she provides, she considers, she plants, she sets, she sees, she holds, she grasps, she opens, she extends, she makes, she supplies, she laughs, she speaks, *and* she watches.

In the meantime, she makes me tired!

However, despite the example she provided, when the lights came up and the credits rolled on this lady's life, my Urge-to-Merge attitude made me stiffen in my seat and spit out my popcorn. Of the twenty-two verses about this woman, *nine* of them make a direct reference to her marital status. That's forty percent of her story that refers to her husband or family or children or household. As for me, I didn't have any of those things. No husband. No household. No handful of kids. Sure, I could still learn a lot from the remaining sixty percent of her story that didn't reference those things, but I still decided to continue my search for a heroine elsewhere.

Ruth

The next woman on my list of possibilities was the faithful and famous Ruth, and she, too, lived up to her reputation. Her story provides an awesome example of commitment and dedication as Ruth clings to her mother-in-law and turns her back on the false gods of her ancestors. Though fresh on the heels of heartache and loss, Ruth refuses to let her newfound status as a widow suck her into the grips of bitterness.

Too bad her story doesn't stop there.

It's not that her story takes a turn for the worse; it doesn't! It's that it takes a turn for the best. As early as chapter 2, Ruth meets the wonderful Boaz, her knight in shining armor, and so begins her second chance at love and marriage.

Dear Diary, Not to sound bitter, but I haven't even had one chance at love and marriage, and this lady gets two!

Sure, I was happy for Ruth, but it was more like the "happy" you feel for the prom queen or for the head cheerleader or for your little sister when she gets married before you. They've all found joy through their rose-colored glasses, and I couldn't help but notice that mine were tinted slightly green. Perhaps I should move on to another possible heroine.

Esther

Esther's story is like the Cinderella fairy tale of the Bible, minus the wicked stepmother and glass slipper. Naturally, it drew this single girl in.

A beauty contest. A year's worth of pampering and beauty treatments. The climax of a royal wedding to a powerful king. It reads more like a modern-day reality series than it does an Old Testament story. (Think *The Bachelor* meets *Extreme Makeover* with a shocking royal twist!)

But beyond the glamour and excitement, I saw in Esther something quite simple and admirable: her willingness to put others before herself. Risking her crown and her life, she used her position as queen to save her people from a potential holocaust. With such a sacrificial heart, the only thing to cast a shadow on Esther's outer poise was the glow of her inner beauty.

But after studying her story, do you think I stopped there? Of course not. The truth remained: I wasn't sure if I'd ever become a wife, let alone a *queen*! So other than my rhinestone tiara, what did I really have in common with this beauty queen, anyway?

The Quest Continues

By now you're probably seeing the same trend that I did when I embarked upon my heroine search. A trend in Scripture that's not usually highlighted from the pulpit. A trend that I wanted desperately to ignore.

So far, it seemed all of the ladies I studied had one small detail in common: they were all *married*! The Proverbs 31 Woman: *married*. Ruth: *married*. Esther: *married*. As a single girl searching for the perfect role model, I'll admit, I had a bit of a problem with this revelation.

Even as I continued my journey, it seemed this trend kept following me like an afternoon shadow. Rahab, the bold and tenacious prostitute from Jericho: *married*. Hannah, the prayer warrior mother of Samuel: *married*. Elizabeth, Rachel, Rebekah, Sarah: *married, married, married, married*.

These ladies were the foundation of my viewpoints on Christian femininity, and gradually it became clear to me that I had less in common with these women than I had originally thought.

Though they all exhibited awesome character in a variety of difficult circumstances—betrayal, war, barrenness, prostitution—none of them had gone through what I was going through: a prolonged

> Finally, that's where *she* came in: The unnamed, unmarried, and unshakable girl in Judges 11 known only as Jephthah's daughter.

and possibly unending period of singleness. Without fail, they were all cemented into history with the same title:

Wife.

I hope I am not the first one to be bothered by this. While their marital status does not negate their credibility, it still left me longing for a role model who shared my status. Someone to teach about being a single woman because she *was* a single woman, not simply because she'd "been there."

Finally, that's where *she* came in: The unnamed, unmarried, and unshakable girl in Judges 11 known only as Jephthah's daughter.

The Heroine Is Discovered

I'd read her story only once before. It's tucked away in between the adventures of Gideon and Samson, so it's easily overshadowed by their action-packed stories. To this day, I've still never even heard a sermon preached about her, and when I ask people to give me their thoughts about the story of Jephthah's daughter, they usually respond with blank stares and crinkled foreheads.

I don't remember when or how I returned to her story during my heroine search, but somehow it became embedded into my heart the first time I read it, and the Lord, in His infinite wisdom, drew me back to it the moment I needed it the most.

My search for a heroine was over.

Immediately, the void that I felt in my heart was filled, and I began reading her story over and over again, sucking in every last detail. I didn't care that the preachers and teachers I'd heard before neglected to share her story from the pulpit. It was enough that I discovered her story at all, and God, I'm sure, had put it there especially for me.

He put her story there for you, too.

God knows what you're going through. He knows that you're searching for a role model and that you're tired of turning to the *Mrs.* Somebody's of the Bible as your only examples. Maybe you've never even pinpointed your frustration before, but now that I've highlighted the marital trend that the other women share, you realize that it has bothered you too. Maybe not overtly, but on some level you've felt the void as well.

Wait no further. You're about to be introduced to the scriptural role model you've been waiting to discover. Chances are, you've probably never read her story before, so here it is, straight from the pages of Judges 11. Ladies, meet Jephthah's daughter ("JD" for short):

> And Jephthah made a vow to the LORD: "If you give the Ammonites into my hands, whatever comes out of the door of my house to meet me when I return in triumph from the Ammonites will be the LORD's, and I will sacrifice it as a burnt offering."
>
> Then Jephthah went over to fight the Ammonites, and the LORD gave them into his hands. He devastated twenty towns from Aroer to the vicinity of Minnith, as far as Abel Keramim. Thus Israel subdued Ammon.
>
> When Jephthah returned to his home in Mizpah, who should come out to meet him but his daughter, dancing to the sound of tambourines! She was an only child. Except for her he had neither son nor daughter. When he saw her, he tore his clothes and cried, "Oh! My daughter! You have made me miserable and wretched, because I have made a vow to the LORD that I cannot break."
>
> "My father," she replied, "you have given your word to the LORD. Do to me just as you promised, now that the LORD has avenged you of your enemies, the Ammonites. But grant me this one request," she said. "Give me two months to roam the hills and weep with my friends, because I will never marry."
>
> "You may go," he said. And he let her go for two months. She and the girls went into the hills and wept because she would never marry. After the two months,

she returned to her father and he did to her as he had vowed. And she was a virgin.

From this comes the Israelite custom that each year the young women of Israel go out for four days to commemorate the daughter of Jephthah the Gileadite (vv. 30–40).

The Controversy: Did He or Didn't He?

After reading this passage just once, you probably have the same question forming in your mind that most do when they hear her story for the first time: *Did he or didn't he?* If your jaw dropped or your eyes widened at the phrase "and he did to her as he had vowed," then congratulations. You've just discovered why this passage is usually avoided from the pulpit.

Obviously, for the sake of this book, the question cannot be avoided. In order to begin studying the story of Jephthah's daughter, we have to address the conclusion of the story and the controversy surrounding it first.

"And he did to her as he had vowed." According to the vow, Jephthah promised the Lord a burnt offering. A sacrifice. Is it possible that Jephthah, JD's own father, actually did . . . *that*?

That's certainly one point of view. Many biblical scholars believe that Jephthah fulfilled his vow in a literal sense by sacrificing JD as a burnt offering. As a (gulp) *human sacrifice*.

Although God forbids human sacrificing in the Old Testament, in the time and place in which Jephthah lived, some say that human sacrificing was a common tradition. While the Israelites were forbidden to participate in this practice, other cultures and religions viewed human sacrificing as a form of worship. And the Israelites had begun to assimilate the traditions of the surrounding cultures.

So if the custom of human sacrificing was not a foreign concept or a shocking possibility at that time, it seems quite likely that Jephthah's daughter became just another unfortunate soul tossed to the fire. Another innocent victim of the flames.

After all, the text *says* he did it. "And he did to her as he had vowed." If the Bible says it, why would you entertain anything but a literal translation of the text?

Some say the argument stops right there. But others disagree.

There is also the point of view that Jephthah did not carry out his vow in a literal sense, but rather in a figurative sense. That he fulfilled the vow in the spirit, not in the letter. According to this viewpoint, the idea is that Jephthah simply committed his daughter to full-time service for the Lord. This way she would never marry and she would never have children. Instead she would be set apart for the Lord as His wholly devoted and totally consecrated servant.

Not a burnt offering, but an offering nonetheless.

Those who believe this option support it by pointing out that JD does not mourn her upcoming death during her two months in the mountains but rather her life of perpetual virginity. Why would she lament her virginity if death were around the corner?

In addition, there is the fact that Jephthah's name appears among the list of Old Testament heroes of faith recorded in Hebrews 11. Since human sacrificing was a pagan form of worship, wouldn't Jephthah's name have been omitted from the honored list of Hebrews if he were guilty of such a scandalous act?

The same verse, two very different interpretations.

Commentaries, pastors, and biblical researchers have debated the explanation of verse 39 for hundreds of years, failing to come to a definitive answer. The verdict is still out, and the jury remains divided.

Did he or didn't he?

For the purpose of this book, I had to form an opinion. I couldn't let the issue go unresolved in an effort to take the easy road out. So after much research and much prayer, I concluded that the text should be understood figuratively. Did Jephthah sacrifice his daughter? Yes. But did he actually tie her up and place her on an altar as a burnt offering? Maybe not.

I have to admit that aside from the research, my Urge to Merge attitude may have influenced my decision a bit. After all, everyone has to face death. For Christians, death promises life! But for a young girl who wanted desperately to get married, to accept a life of perpetual virginity with no hope of marriage *ever*—that was a person I could look up to. There were times I thought I might welcome death over the alternative of becoming an "old maid," and as ridiculous as that statement sounds, Jephthah's daughter always helped bring me to my senses during those times.

You may agree or disagree with the opinion that Jephthah did not actually kill his daughter, but I urge you in either case to look past the unanswered questions embedded in this story and focus on the bigger picture. Don't get so distracted by the heroine's destiny that the most important lesson, the heroine's character, gets buried in controversy.

Scholars and single girls alike may still debate about *how* Jephthah's daughter was sacrificed, but the bottom line remains undisputed: JD *was* sacrificed.

Lessons from a Heroine

After getting past the initial shock of JD's story, you can see why I connected so naturally with her. She could have easily been present at my last slumber party or at my last small group meeting or been the voice at the other end of my cell phone on a dateless Saturday night.

Every now and then, you meet someone who is going through life at about the same pace as you are, and instantly you become lifelong friends. Such moments and such friends are rare, to say the least, but whenever you find them, you never feel more blessed.

Jephthah's daughter is such a friend to me.

I can't wait to get to heaven one day and meet her. After my Savior and my family, this girl is the first one I want to see. We'll go to Starbucks (because I'm sure there's a franchise in heaven too), and we'll talk for hours over coffee and cappuccino, with our giggles drowning out the smooth and mellow music that dances in the atmosphere.

I'll ask her what *really* happened, of course. But more than that, I'll ask her how she did it. *How did you maintain such unwavering faith and character when your deepest desire, the desire to be married, was abruptly crushed through no fault of your own?*

How did you do it, JD?

How could you still speak to God under such unfair circumstances?

How could you still love your father when he used your marital status as a negotiating tool?

How did you keep from getting jealous of your friends when they all became brides and you remained a bridesmaid?

Tell me how you did it, JD, and pass the non-fat cream and sweetener while you're at it.

You see, that is what makes Jephthah's daughter different from other singles in the Bible. Unlike Paul, who spoke of marriage as a distraction he'd rather not have to deal with, JD saw marriage as something to look forward to. She wanted to get married; she *longed* to get married. And when her deepest desire went no further than catching the bouquet at a friend's wedding, she didn't try to mask her disappointment with an empty laugh and a fake smile. Instead, she cried.

> Instead, the heroine finds comfort in the mountains, support from her non-dwarf friends, and strength that comes not from a potion, but from her heavenly Father.

She wept. She *lamented.* And her tears are what I connected with the most.

I've wept before. I've lamented.

And I'm sure you have too.

Pull up a chair. JD's just about to tell us how she did it!

Over the next ten chapters, as we dig deeper into the story of Jephthah's daughter, you're going to discover a fairy tale unlike one you've ever heard before. Though it begins "once upon a time" and ends "happily every after," there are no magic fairies to hide the heroine from her destiny, no singing mice to accompany her tambourine playing, and, most significantly, no Prince Charming to fulfill what she believes to be her deepest desires. Instead, the heroine finds comfort in the mountains, support from her non-dwarf friends, and strength that comes not from a potion, but from her heavenly Father.

Together, we'll look at **her gumption** and redefine our own independence. We'll study **her genes**, thereby exploring the significance of our own heritage. **Her grace** will teach us the importance of reaching out to others, while **her grasp** of Scripture will amaze us and emphasize our own need to study God's Word.

A look at her relationship with **her God** will show us the value of worship, and by getting to know **her girls,** we'll be reminded of the value of friendship. **Her grief** and **her guarantee** will illustrate the fine line between expressing our emotions and allowing our emotions to control our actions.

Finally, studying **her guiltlessness** will highlight the value of purity in our own lives, while a glimpse of **her guidance** will inspire us to serve God in every circumstance.

And now, a closer look at our heroine's fairy tale begins with an introduction that could quite possibly begin your own fairy tale:

Once upon a time, there was a spirited and beautiful woman. And though she was single, she longed to be married...

Your Heroine Search

1. Who is your favorite female Bible character, and why? What lessons have you learned from her?

2. Other than Bible characters, who serves as a female role model for you, and why?

3. What is your first impression of Jephthah?

4. What is your first impression of Jephthah's daughter?

5. The controversy of Judges 11:39, "and he did to her as he had vowed," is probably a big reason the story of Jephthah's daughter is not taught more often. While either interpretation leads to an undesirable outcome, which fate do you think would be harder to endure: dying young or living a long life as an "old maid"? In your opinion, which outcome do you think JD had to endure, and why?

6. Before today, have you ever heard a sermon or read a book that mentioned Jephthah or his daughter? If so, what do you remember about the lesson?

7. Of the ten aspects of JD's character that we will be looking at in part 2 of this book, which attribute are you looking forward to studying the most? Why?

8. ***Memorize*** Proverbs 31:29–30: "Many women do noble things, but you surpass them all. Charm is deceptive, and beauty is fleeting; but a woman who fears the Lord is to be praised."

Part Two

UNNAMED

Chapter 3

Her Gumption

When Jephthah returned to his home in Mizpah, who should come out to meet him but his daughter, dancing to the sound of tambourines! (Judges 11:34).

The Sounds of Music

When you think of the different types of music, you probably stick to the basic categories: country, rock, jazz, oldies, and rap. But when I think of music, my category list tends to be a little more specific. For me, there's driving music, cleaning music, music that goes great with coffee, music that sounds better in the fall, road-trip music, Saturday morning music, breakup music, and the list goes on.

If that's not crazy enough, I also tend to remember different periods of my life by the "soundtrack" I've associated with them. There's the soundtrack to my junior high cheerleading days, complete with dance music, fight songs, and a couple of early

nineties ballads to keep things "real." There's the soundtrack
to high school featuring a handful of cheesy love songs. Then
there's the college summer soundtrack that I literally threw out
the window of my car somewhere between Huntsville and Van,
Texas, during an overdramatic post-breakup drive in the rain.

> And I know that every time I hear a tambourine, I think of Jephthah's daughter.

Ah, the power of the mixed CD.

I may not be a musician, and I may never have taken
a course in music theory, but I still have a few music theories of
my own.

Aside from music being one of the most motivational, inspi-
rational, and emotional venues in existence, it is also one of the
best reflections of God's creativity. It is diverse enough that it
can please children, adults, the poor, the rich, the educated, and
the uneducated, yet it is universal enough that it can cross lan-
guage barriers, hurdle geographical walls, and bridge the ocean
of time.

That sounds like the beginning of some promising song lyrics
right there. Okay, maybe not.

The truth is, I can't explain the power of music. And I don't
know why it affects us like it does. I only know that the theme
song from *Indiana Jones* made my college roommate gallop
around our living room and that anything by Kenny G makes
me want to light candles and draw a bath.

And I know that every time I hear a tambourine, I think of
Jephthah's daughter.

Her Theme Song, Her Gumption

In the first picture we have of JD, she's running out to greet her father, dancing and shaking her tambourine. I picture her barefooted, with a long, flowing skirt that swishes as she sways. Her dark, unruly hair cascades past her shoulders and mirrors the movements of her skirt. She probably runs out so quickly, she doesn't even bother to shut the door behind her. And as she twirls and spins in celebration, she holds her tambourine high above her head as she shakes it with one hand and gently beats it with the palm of the other.

It's an image of joy and happiness. And somehow the core of her character is revealed in this initial image of JD dancing to her tambourine. Her energy. Her pizzazz. Her spirit. Her gumption. All growing louder and clearer with each shake, rattle, and roll.

Now, be honest. Would you get the same first impression if she were to come out of the house playing, let's see, a tuba perhaps?

Probably not.

What about an oboe or a violin or the bagpipes maybe? I tried picturing every instrument I could possibly think of in place of the tambourine in this story, and nothing else fits. It's like trying to picture the Boogie Woogie Bugle Boy with a cello. Or the Little Drummer Boy with a trombone. It doesn't work. Only the tambourine fits the story of Jephthah's daughter.

But it's no wonder, because the tambourine always shows up in Scripture as an instrument of celebration. An instrument of praise!

After the Israelites fled from Egypt and all of Pharaoh's army was swallowed by the Red Sea, a tambourine medley underscored their victory. "Then Miriam the prophetess, Aaron's sister, took a tambourine in her hand, and all the women followed her, with tambourines and dancing" (Exodus 15:20).

After David killed Goliath, the sound of tambourines again rang out. "When the men were returning home after David had killed the Philistine, the women came out from all the towns of Israel to meet King Saul with singing and dancing, with joyful songs and with tambourines and lutes" (1 Samuel 18:6).

Again David celebrated with tambourines after the Ark of the Covenant was brought to Jerusalem. "David and the whole house of Israel were celebrating with all their might before the LORD, with songs and with harps, lyres, tambourines, sistrums and cymbals" (2 Samuel 6:5).

I like that description. They were celebrating *with all their might*.

When was the last time you celebrated something with all your might? And when was the last time you put it to music?

You're probably like most people and haven't touched a tambourine since elementary school music class. I encourage you to change that.

The tambourine is a *happy* instrument. To my knowledge, you can't play the tambourine and remain melancholy. First, you shake it a few times. Then you throw in a tap every now and then for a shake-tap-shake, shake-tap-shake. And before you know it, your hips have joined in on the shaking, your feet have joined in on the tapping, and you're outright dancing to the sound of a tambourine! You're spinning. You're swaying. You're dancing. You're shaking!

Just like Jephthah's daughter.

Unfortunately, this is only the beginning of her story, and despite this bright and cheery opening scene, we can't deny the tragic turn of events that is about to take place. But we can remember one thing: The tambourine is not just the overture of JD's story; it's her theme song.

As we continue to study this unnamed, unmarried, and unshakable woman, I want you to constantly keep the sound of the tambourine at the forefront of your mind. Remember it. *Hear* it. And let it be a reminder of her first notable character trait—her gumption—as the story unfolds.

The Instrument of Identity

One of the reasons that JD's tambourine sounds so sweet is that she was a tambourine player.

That may sound like an obvious statement, but it's often the first truth that we single girls trip on. We're tambourine players, and yet we spend most of our time wishing we were pianists instead. Or cellists. Or drummers.

If that doesn't make sense, what about this: We're single, and yet we spend most of our time wishing we were married instead. Or engaged. Or dating.

In order to become a woman of gumption, you must first discover what instrument you were created to play. Your instrument is, in a sense, your identity.

That's not always easy to pinpoint, especially for girls. *Identity.* Who *am* I? And single girls have it even harder because we feel like even if we figure out who we are right now, it could all change if and when we get married. After all, our names will change, won't they? And when we set our minds on the possibility of changing our names some day, it makes it that much easier to think of ourselves as two different people. The single me and the married me. Emily Elizabeth Maricelli, and Emily Elizabeth *To Be Determined*. Two different names, two different identities. Right?

Wrong.

The first thing we have to realize is that a name change does not constitute an identity change. Who we are right now is who we are. Period. Our names do not define us. Our marital status does not define us.

> The Bible says that you don't need to find *yourself* at all; you need to seek God.

In fact, *we* don't define ourselves at all.

Of course that's not what the world says. The world says that if you're having an identity crisis, you need to go out and "find yourself."

The Bible says that you don't need to find *yourself* at all; you need to seek God. "But seek first his kingdom and his righteousness, and all these things will be given to you as well" (Matthew 6:33).

We're foolish to look inward in an attempt to discover who we are. Only God knows exactly who we are, because He is the One who created us. Psalm 139:13 says that He created our *inmost being*. That's the very part of us that most people go searching for.

Our inmost being. Our identity.

Jephthah's daughter knew her identity. She was a tambourine player. And because she knew *who* she was, she also knew *what* she was to do.

Waiting for the Lord

If we're not careful, we could focus solely on the fact that JD shook her tambourine and skip past all of the other things that reflect her gumption. It's true that JD knew her identity, but she also knew her *activity*.

Judges 11:34 says that when Jephthah came home, "Who should come out to meet him but his daughter!" Such a simple statement, but it raises all sorts of questions in my mind. How did she know her father was coming? Why wasn't she with her father? What was she doing while she was inside? How did she know her father's army had been victorious?

By taking a deeper look at this opening scene, we get a better grasp on what she was doing before the first shake of her tambourine.

For starters, there was a war going on. The Israelites were at war with the Ammonites, and unlike today, the battlefield was an estrogen-free zone. Women didn't go to the frontlines like they do today. They remained at home to keep house while the men were away. JD knew that her father's place was in battle and hers was at home, so that's exactly where she was.

On the surface, this may sound like a boring life. The men are out making a difference while the women are at home making beds. The men get to see the action while the women get to wait.

That doesn't sound glamorous to me. Waiting.

For singles, that's sometimes the scariest four-letter word ever: *wait*. You pray to meet someone special. God says *wait*. You pray to become a wife. God says *wait*. You pray to start a family. God says *wait*.

Just between you and me, don't you ever get tired of waiting? Waiting implies inaction. It suggests remaining in a stagnant state for an undetermined length of time. We can't speed up waiting. We can't test out of it. *All* we can do is wait . . .

And wait . . .

And wait . . .

The hardest part about waiting is that we don't know what to do *while* we're waiting. If we could just do something to take our minds off the fact that we're waiting, maybe it wouldn't seem to go by so slowly.

Because this was such a difficult concept for me to grasp—knowing what to do while I waited—I finally sat down one day and had a talk with God. "God, I know I have to wait on You. I fought it for a long time, but I've accepted it now. But what do I do in the meantime?"

He answered, "Wait on Me."

"God, I got that part. Didn't you just hear me? I said that I've accepted the fact that I'm supposed to wait on You. Just tell me what to do *while* I'm waiting."

Again He answered, "Wait."

"So you want me to wait while I wait?"

"Yes."

"God, I love You, and I don't want to sound disrespectful, but that's crazy! How can I wait while I wait?"

And He just smiled (that's how I pictured it, anyway) and said again, "Just wait. You'll see soon enough what I mean."

It took a shoe sale to finally make me understand what God was saying. After a sales lady brought me a huge stack of shoes, all in my size and all on sale, and laid them at my feet, it hit me.

All this time I was thinking of the usual definition of the word *wait: to stay in one place or do nothing until something happens or in the expectation or hope that something will happen.*

That's not what God wants us to do at all. We're forgetting that there's a second definition of the word *wait: to be ready or available for somebody to take or use.* To *wait* on someone is *to serve* someone. Butlers wait on their employers. Waiters wait tables. Salespeople wait on shoppers. There's nothing stagnant or inactive about any one of those.

God says, "Wait on Me while you wait on Me." In other words, "Serve Me while you wait. Be active while you wait."

Suddenly, waiting on God didn't seem boring at all.

> Wait for the Lord! It's not a dreaded sentencing; it's a call to action!

When JD was waiting for her father to come back from battle, she wasn't sitting around twiddling her thumbs. She was taking care of things. She was keeping the house clean. She was cooking. She was tending to the animals. She was active.

We know this because Jephthah didn't come home to a long list of things that had gone wrong in his absence. Instead he came home to a celebration. Everything was on track. Everything was ready for him. Break out the dinner mints and grab a tambourine—it's time for a party!

Psalm 27:14 says, "Wait for the LORD; be strong and take heart and wait for the LORD." I used to read this verse and grimace. It sounded so dull and boring and pious. After all, it is a stereotypical "encouragement" for singles. "Don't worry, honey *[insert patronizing pat on the head here].* God will bring you a husband in His own time. Just wait for the Lord."

Gag.

However, now that God has helped me redefine the word *wait*, this verse sounds more like a battle cry to me than it does a superfluous suggestion.

Wait for the Lord! It's not a dreaded sentencing; it's a call to action!

Woman of Independence

Not only did Jephthah's daughter know *who* she was (her identity), and *what* to do (her activity), she also knew *how* to do it.

On first glance, this looks like her independence. That's what I thought it was the first hundred or so times I read her story. This girl has got it all together. She knows how to run things while her father is away. She doesn't need anyone by her side telling her what to do. If her story was set in modern times, I think JD would look like a lot of us.

She'd not only have a college degree, she'd also have put herself through school and graduated with honors. She'd be able to live with roommates but would be totally comfortable living alone. She'd be able to juggle a full-time career with volunteering at her church and still have time to train for a marathon and maintain an active social life. You go, girl! Way to be an independent woman!

But the truth is, that's not how all of us look. Sure, it's how we *want* to look. We want to have it all together. We want to be self-sufficient. There's something admirable about being independent. About not needing a man. About not needing anyone!

Even some Christian circles teach independence to singles. You don't need a mate. You have more time and energy to serve

God when you're not married. You're complete without a better half.

But while all of those things are true, if you don't put it into the right context, independence can be very dangerous territory.

I tried to exercise my independence a few years ago when I bought my very first "real" bed. For some reason, that was a purchase I always expected to make with my fiancé someday. Together we'd pick out the perfect bed to go with all of the bedroom decor we'd registered for, we'd set it up in our new house, and neither of us would sleep on it until we returned home from our honeymoon. That was just the way it was supposed to be. But when I realized that I was in my mid-twenties and had never slept in anything but a twin-sized bed, I finally gave up the dream, and the independent woman in me went furniture shopping.

I choked back tears as I zigzagged through the showcase floor of the furniture store. I kept my head down and focused on the mattresses and nightstands in order to avoid making eye contact with the overzealous sales associates eager to meet my furnishing needs. They might be able to sell me a bed, but none of them knew what I really wanted.

Sure, I wanted a new bed. I wouldn't be getting out my tape measure and flipping over price tags if I didn't. But I never imagined my first venture out of the world of twin-sized mattresses would be like this. That it would be under these circumstances. That I would feel more defeated than excited.

That I would be alone.

Let's face it. We've all seen the commercials. Single girls don't buy beds. *Couples* buy beds.

First they walk hand in hand throughout the store, surveying the entire collection at once. Then the wife pauses by a gorgeous queen-sized mattress and brushes her free hand gently across the fluffy quilted pillow top. The husband walks around to the other side and plops down on the potential purchase, fully noticing how the bounce accepts his weight. He is pleased. He pats the mattress beside him and beckons his wife to judge for herself.

Finally, there they both are. Lying on their backs, side by side, making subtle snow angels with their hands as they imagine the mattress in their home. In their bedroom. Dressed in their five-hundred-thread-count Egyptian cotton sheets.

It's never the single girl walking around the furniture store on a Saturday afternoon in her T-shirt and sweat pants. Just once I'd like to see a commercial that told the story that way.

After all, that was the way it was for me.

Even when I signed the papers for my gorgeous new queen-sized sleigh bed, I still didn't feel like a conquering, self-made independent woman. If anything, I felt kind of lonely.

Again, I sat down and had a talk with God. "God, if I'm not supposed to be independent, but I'm not supposed to be dependent on a man either, where does that leave me?"

And again He gave me the same sort of cryptic answer as before. He said, "Seek in dependence."

Instead of arguing, I pondered His words this time. "So *independence* is out of the question, but *in dependence* is the way to go?"

"Exactly," He said.

"Since we live by the Spirit, let us keep in step with the Spirit" (Galatians 5:25). True *in dependence* is not walking on your own. Rather it's accepting Christ and walking *in* complete *dependence* of the Holy Spirit—the One who guides your steps.

Watching the Conductor

Exercising godly independence is like playing in an orchestra. Let's say that you have an instrument—a tambourine, perhaps—and you play in an eighty-piece orchestra. If everyone sat down and independently started playing his or her instrument, it would probably sound awful. Everything would sound chaotic and unrehearsed, and even the best musicians in the world would get drowned out by the commotion. Likewise, if only one person played at a time, it would sound like something was missing. There would be holes of silence in the song that would make that musician's music feel empty.

That's why orchestras have conductors. The conductor leads the group to play in perfect sync with each other. He determines the tempo, the volume, everything. Each musician may be playing independently of the other, but all are dependent on the conductor. They shake when he says shake and beat when he says beat.

And that's how great music is played.

The problem with typical independence is that it forgets about the conductor, and it crumbles when it's threatened. The very thing that makes independence what it is is that it stands alone. It has no outside variables to factor into the equation. Only if you lived in a bubble could you be truly independent, because other people interfere with our lives every day. Careless drivers rear-end us at the stoplight. Parents disappoint us. Boys break up with us.

On first glance, JD looks like a girl of great independence, and I still don't doubt that this girl could hold her own. But when we dig deeper, we realize that what she had was not independence at all. It was complete dependence on God.

If JD were an "independent woman," she would have fought back when someone—namely, her father—ruined her hopes and dreams. Instead, as we'll see in future chapters, her character, her gumption, was unwavering.

Independence is way too fragile to withstand a story like JD's. Only dependence on God remains steady when unforeseen circumstances arise.

Your Theme Song, Your Gumption

So how's your gumption? If your life were a movie, what would be your theme song? Would it be similar to the never-give-up beat of *Rocky*? Or the tragic piano tunes of *Love Story*?

Or would it be more like JD's theme song, with constant tambourine shakes that reflect your energy? Your pizzazz. Your gumption.

When you read JD's story and think, *I can't put my finger on it, but there's something about this girl I really like,* that's her gumption. It's a combination of her identity, her activity, and her *in dependence.*

Gumption is discovering that your identity has nothing to do with who you are and everything to do with who God is.

Gumption is understanding that waiting on God is an active task, not a passive one.

Gumption is not becoming an independent woman, but becoming a woman solely dependent on Christ.

So, how's your gumption?

Your Gumption

1. What songs would be on the soundtrack to your life, and why? How would your theme song sound?

2. Which do you struggle with the most: knowing who you are (your identity), knowing what to do with your life (your activity), or depending on God to guide you (your "in dependence")?

3. Read Psalm 139:1–16. What does God know about you? If you could, what part of your inmost being would you hide from Him?

4. Are you currently waiting on God by serving Him? If not, what is keeping you from doing so? Read Ephesians 2:10 to find one of the reasons you were created. What are some ways that you can wait on the Lord in your church? In your community?

5. What does Proverbs 3:5–6 suggest about independence versus "in dependence"? Are there any areas in your life that you are still living independently from God? If so, what might it take for you to become dependent on God in those areas?

6. Read about praising God in Psalm 150. *Why* should we praise God? *How* should we praise God? Finally, *who* should praise God?

7. What reasons did JD have for praising God with her tambourine in this opening scene? What reasons do you have for praising God today?

8. *Memorize* Psalm 139:13–14b: "For you created my inmost being; you knit me together in my mother's womb. I praise you because I am fearfully and wonderfully made."

Chapter 4

Her Genes

She was an only child. Except for her he had neither son
nor daughter (Judges 11:34).

I'd Like to Exchange These Genes, Please

I was fifteen when I discovered that my father is not perfect. That may seem a little old to you, or it may seem a little
young, depending on your relationship with your own father.
Nevertheless, until that time, my dad enjoyed a secure and quite
comfortable position at the top of the pedestal on which I kept
him.

It started when something amazing happened—James Davis
asked me out! We were both on the student drama team at
church, and while he was always nice, I never dreamed he'd actually like me. After all, he was a junior and I was a freshman.
And not only was he an awesome Christian, he was also the most
good-looking guy in the entire youth group and unknowingly

made half of the girls at church, including me, go weak in the knees every time he was around.

My knees were downright quaking the Sunday he asked me to meet him in the hall after church. And when he invited me on a double date with him and another couple, I knew that my knees would no longer be a problem—I was, after all, *floating* the entire way home.

I explained to him that I wasn't allowed to date until I turned sixteen in October, but he respectfully offered to call my dad himself and request an exception be made this once. The phone call came that very evening, but despite my highest hopes, my father still said no. It didn't matter that James was a complete gentleman when they spoke on the phone. It didn't make a difference that I was just a few months shy of the "magic" age of sixteen. And it didn't matter how many tears I could muster. Dad's *no* was unwavering.

That was the day that my dad slipped off his pedestal, awkwardly tumbling down in a very Humpty Dumpty-like fashion, and remained at the bottom for the rest of the summer. By fall, James Davis had moved away, and our romance ended before it ever even had a chance to begin. I approached my sixteenth birthday wishing, as every sixteen-year-old wishes at one time or another, that I could exchange my genes for some with a little more "relaxed fit."

Unraveling the Family Ties

I suppose this story in Judges marks the point at which Jephthah fell off his pedestal too. No doubt JD had placed him there at an early age. Most little girls put their daddies on pedestals at some point in their lives. And, much to the chagrin of their daughters, all fathers eventually find the Humpty-Dumpty way off those pedestals.

So in order to learn more about Jephthah's daughter, it makes sense that we must also learn more about Jephthah. After all, in the three chapters it takes to tell Jephthah's story, only seven of those verses actually account for JD's cameo.

So who was Jephthah before this key passage in Judges 11? What kind of relationship did he have with his daughter? With the rest of his family? With his God?

Jephthah lived in the time after the death of Joshua but before the beginning of the monarchy known as the period of the judges. The Israelites, finally living in the Promised Land, seemed stuck in an endless cycle of rebellion and repentance recorded throughout the book of Judges. Time and time again, the cycle would repeat:

- *Rebellion*: The Israelites disobeyed God, worshiped false gods, and did evil in the eyes of the Lord.
- *Retribution*: God, in His anger, would hand the Israelites over to one of their enemies.
- *Repentance*: After some soul searching, the Israelites at last turned back to God.
- *Rescue*: God gave them another chance and sent them a judge to save them from their enemies.
- *Rest*: Throughout the judge's lifetime, the nation enjoyed a time of peace as they followed and obeyed God.

Rebellion. Retribution. Repentance. Rescue. Rest. Twelve times this cycle occurred, and twelve times God sent a judge to save the Israelites and give them another chance.

Jephthah was one of these judges.

He makes a notable first impression at his biblical debut. Judges 11:1 introduces him as "a mighty warrior" (NIV), while other Bible versions describe him as "a brave warrior" or "a mighty man of valor."

With an introduction like that, how could his little girl look at him with anything but childlike adoration?

Because of his reputation as a great warrior, Jephthah was the first one the Israelites ran to when they found themselves under attack by the Ammonites. The nation needed saving. The nation needed leadership.

The nation needed a hero.

I'm sure JD was proud of her father when he left to lead the Israelites. She probably prepared food for him to take with him on his journey. She probably listened intently as he explained what needed to be done to keep their home in order during his absence. And as he bent down and kissed her cheek with his final goodbye, she probably promised to pray for his safety and for victory in battle.

"Don't worry. I'll be back soon," he probably said as he noticed the single tear that somehow escaped from his daughter's strong eyes.

JD, Your Roots Are Showing

The bond between a father and a daughter can be strong even under normal circumstances. But, in this case, I believe that the bond was even stronger than usual.

The Bible is clear on the fact that JD was an only child. "Except for her, [Jephthah] had neither son nor daughter" (Judges 11:34).

Since JD's mother is never mentioned in Scripture, it's possible that Jephthah was the only immediate family member that JD had.

When we read the rest of verses 1 and 2, we discover an extended family that is anything but picture perfect. Naturally, every family tree has its cracked branches, but JD's family tree seems to sprout leaves of betrayal and dysfunction rather than of love and godly living.

Her grandmother, for starters, was not the typical granny. While most of JD's friends probably had grandmothers who passed down family heirlooms and taught them how to knit and maintain the perfect garden, JD's grandmother was known for something quite different.

She was a prostitute.

Add to that the fact that JD's grandfather, Gilead, was a married man when

> With no one else around to usurp his position as his little girl's hero, Jephthah's place on his daughter's pedestal was unshakable.

he sought the services of the prostitute, and you have a patriarch who was a first-class adulterer.

They don't sound like the type of grandparents that Hallmark makes cards for, do they?

Their indiscretion resulted in Jephthah's birth, which labeled him from the womb as an illegitimate child and an automatic social outcast. Even his own half-brothers, JD's uncles, drove Jephthah away and refused to see him as part of the family.

Adultery. Prostitution. Abandonment. Rejection. The sum of which leads us back to Jephthah and JD, all alone except for each other. A father-daughter bond strengthened if for no other reason than by the lack of anyone else to cling to. With no one else around to usurp his position as his little girl's hero, Jephthah's place on his daughter's pedestal was unshakable.

Well, almost.

A Hero's Faith

We've already speculated in the previous chapter about what JD was doing while her father was away at war. She was actively waiting for him to return, following the orders he'd left for her and anticipating his victorious return. The Bible gives a much more detailed account of this time from Jephthah's point of view, for it is during this time that Jephthah not only shines as a mighty man of valor, he also shines as a mighty man of faith as well.

In three quick passages, we can see the heart and character of Jephthah revealed. First, even though he was swept up into this newfound position as Israel's judge, he never forgot that the true Judge of Israel, the One who ultimately decides the fate of a nation and that of its enemies, is the Lord.

"Let the LORD, the Judge, decide the dispute this day between the Israelites and the Ammonites" (v. 27). Even though he was a great warrior, Jephthah knew that battles alone do not win a war. "Let the Lord decide," he said. Not battles. Not politics. Not logic. Not chance.

Let the Lord, the ultimate Judge, decide.

Second, Jephthah experienced a unique empowering by the Holy Spirit, thereby reaffirming God's hand upon him. "Then the Spirit of the LORD came upon Jephthah" (v. 29). In the Old Testament, this unique touch was given to a handful of individuals, enabling them to carry out certain responsibilities that God had given to them. Jephthah experienced this special touch, proving that the hand of the Lord was most certainly on him.

But perhaps the most telling bit of information concerning Jephthah's character is not even found in the book of Judges. It is found in the New Testament in a passage written hundreds of years after Jephthah's lifetime.

Hebrews 11, also known as the "Hall of Faith" chapter of the Bible, gives a list of reputable believers in the past who, by faith, did amazing things. People like Abraham, Isaac, Jacob, and Joseph are just a few mentioned in this chapter. And among these pillars of faith stands JD's father, Jephthah. "And what more shall I say? I do not have time to tell about Gideon, Barak, Samson, Jephthah, David, Samuel and the prophets, who through faith conquered kingdoms, administered justice, and gained what was promised" (vv. 32–33).

Jephthah was indeed a man of great faith. But just like many of the men of faith chronicled in Hebrews 11, even his faith did not stop him from making an unfortunate mistake— a mistake that would cost him more than he ever imagined.

A mistake that would cost him his daughter.

Daddy's Little Girl

If JD was proud of her father when he left for battle, I'm sure she was *ecstatic* when he returned. In her mind, her father was probably at the highest point of respect and admiration he'd ever attained after leading the Israelites to victory over the Ammonites. He rose above his dysfunctional family to become a mighty warrior. He traded his position as a social outcast for that of a national leader. And he succeeded in freeing his people from eighteen years of oppression.

His pedestal had never been higher.

If only verses 30 and 31 had never taken place. "And Jephthah made a vow to the LORD: 'If you give the Ammonites into my hands, whatever comes out of the door of my house to meet me when I return in triumph from the Ammonites will be the LORD's, and I will sacrifice it as a burnt offering.'"

How many times, I wonder, did Jephthah regret saying those words?

And what motivated Jephthah to make such a vow anyway? Was it made in a moment of panic like the desperate cries made in the trenches of Vietnam or on the beaches of Normandy? Or did Jephthah simply not think before he spoke?

If anything, where was his faith that he was known for in Hebrews 11? "*If* you give the Ammonites into my hands"? Why did he ever doubt that God would do what He promised?

When JD ran out to greet her heroic father, shaking her tambourine and unknowingly sealing her fate, I wonder how long it took her to notice the wave of shock that swept across her father's eyes. How long until she noticed that his face, though tanned in battle, had suddenly turned pale? How long did it take her to realize that her daddy, who should have been thrilled to see her, was not even smiling?

In Scripture it all comes out pretty quickly. Jephthah promised a sacrifice, and the sacrifice had been chosen. JD, Daddy's little girl, would pay the price for her father's tragic vow.

I'm sure the consequences of his vow did not escape his mind when the realization hit him. They probably rushed his thoughts all at once, detail after horrifying detail, as he entertained the empty wish that he could somehow turn back time.

Because of his vow, JD would never get married. She would never know the joy of becoming a wife, and Jephthah would never have the honor of giving her away in marriage. Because of him, she would never experience the blessings of motherhood, and Jephthah would never know the thrill of becoming a grandfather. Because of him, his little girl would never see her deepest desires fulfilled.

And it was all his fault.

To say that Jephthah slipped off his pedestal that day would be an understatement. It was more like he came crashing down, along the way crushing dreams, smashing hopes, and landing on the reality that he, like all of our fathers, is not perfect.

Designer Genes

"Where is the hope?" you may ask. In this story of a seemingly unbreakable father-daughter bond so suddenly and so easily ripped apart by betrayal, how can there be any good news left to salvage in the rubble?

In the last chapter, you got to know JD. You probably identified with the young spirited girl, and now you are crushed by the actions of her father.

How *could* he?

Perhaps you even see a little bit of yourself in her. The potential. The spunk. The gumption. You might recognize these promising qualities in yourself and be concerned that all of your strengths are not enough to protect you from the weaknesses of another.

You can also relate to JD because your father, like hers and like mine, has fallen off his pedestal too.

He may have tripped off, slipped off, slid off, or bungee-jumped off, but the little girl in you remembers a time, either in reality or in your imagination, when his pedestal stood higher than it does right now. So what is the good news? The good news is that we have a Father who sits not on a pedestal, but on a throne!

> **The good news is that we have a Father who sits not on a pedestal, but on a throne!**

And because of Jesus, we have the hope of a *new* Father-daughter relationship with a Daddy who will never let us down!

Galatians 4:4–5 says that God sent Jesus to redeem us so that through Him we might experience our rightful heritage. We don't have to be ruled by the imperfections of our earthly families, because we can be adopted into God's family. We can become children of God. We can become *His* daughters. "Because you are [daughters], God sent the Spirit of his Son into our hearts, the Spirit who calls out, '*Abba*, Father.' So you are no longer a slave, but a [daughter]" (Galatians 4:6–7).

With God as your Father, you are no longer a slave to a history of broken homes. You are no longer a slave to parental relationships turned sour. You are no longer a slave to the shortcomings you've inherited from your family.

In fact, you are no longer a slave to your genes at all.

God, the Creator and Designer of the universe, gives us *new* genes. Genes of righteousness through Christ. Genes that don't fade in the washing machine of life. Genes that don't shrink in hot water.

He gives us *Designer* genes.

JD and Jephthah had a father-daughter bond that was broken because her father wasn't perfect. But JD had faith in the knowledge that her *real* Father-daughter bond, the bond she had with her heavenly Father, could *never* be broken.

Romans 8:38–39 tells us, "neither death nor life, neither angels nor demons, neither the present nor the future, nor any powers, neither height nor depth, nor anything else in all creation, will be able to separate us from the love of God that is in Christ Jesus our Lord."

I'd like to add a few more conditions to that list.

Neither good parents nor bad parents.

Neither a Christian home nor an unChristian home.

Neither being single nor being married can separate you from the love God has for you, His little girl.

God, your Heavenly Father, knows how to love you.

And if that's not enough, the good news keeps getting better. God not only loves His children, He also promises them an awesome inheritance! "Now if we are children, then we are heirs—heirs of God and co-heirs with Christ" (Romans 8:17).

God's children receive an inheritance only God's Son could orchestrate—the inheritance of eternal life!

1 Peter 1:3–4 says that our eternal inheritance is a "new birth," a "living hope," and "an inheritance that can never perish, spoil or fade—kept in heaven for you."

I hope you got that last part: kept in heaven for *you*.

Tomato Heirs

My parents have a house on Lake Livingston in east Texas next door to a very kind retired fisherman named Dave. Every year, during tomato season, I would stare longingly into Dave's garden, and my mouth would water for a handful of his homegrown cherry tomatoes. I never trespassed into his garden myself, but sometimes my father would pick a bowl full of tomatoes and share them with me. I'd pop the tiny tomatoes into my mouth like candy and relish in the purity of their taste, devoid of any hints of pesticide residue that normally tarnish the grocery store tomatoes.

One summer I was with my dad when he picked a few luscious tomatoes for each of us, and I commented on the generosity of Neighbor Dave to share his garden with us. My dad wiped the tomato juice from his chin and laughed. "This isn't Dave's garden," he said. "This is *my* garden."

I was stunned. "It is?" I asked.

"Of course it is. Dave just takes care of it since we're not here all the time. And since it's my garden, I guess that makes it your garden too. You can have all the tomatoes you want!"

It was as if he had offered me gold or jewels! "You mean that after all these years of admiring this garden from afar, fighting cravings and settling for second-rate store-bought tomatoes, I could have been eating *these* the whole time?"

He gave me a wink and another tomato. "I guess it helps to know who your father is, doesn't it?"

Do you know who your Father is? Not your earthly father, who may or may not have a tomato garden. But your heavenly Father, who has acre upon acre of blessings and promises for you to claim. How well do you really know Him?

Because we are His children, we are also His heirs. But how are we ever to claim our inheritance unless we get to know our

Father? Our Father's garden contains anything we could ever need to sustain us in this life. Rows and rows of wisdom are available to us whenever we crave it. Fields of forgiveness stretch past the horizon. And trees of love bear their fruit year-round, with roots so deep they could never be unearthed.

Knowing your Father means knowing the fruit—the promises—He offers to His children:

- *Comfort:* "Blessed are those who mourn, for they will be comforted" (Matthew 5:4).
- *Companionship:* "Come near to God and he will come near to you" (James 4:8).
- *Direction:* "I will instruct you and teach you in the way you should go; I will counsel you and watch over you" (Psalm 32:8).
- *Forgiveness:* "If we confess our sins, he is faithful and just and will forgive us our sins and purify us from all unrighteousness" (1 John 1:9).
- *Joy:* "I have told you this so that my joy may be in you and that your joy may be complete" (John 15:11).
- *Rest:* "Come to me, all you who are weary and burdened, and I will give you rest" (Matthew 11:28).
- *Security:* "What, then, shall we say in response to this? If God is for us, who can be against us?" (Romans 8:31).
- *Wisdom:* "If any of you lacks wisdom, he should ask God, who gives generously to all without finding fault, and it will be given to him" (James 1:5).

And many others. "Every good and perfect gift is from above, coming down from the Father of the heavenly lights, who does not change like shifting shadows" (James 1:17). Don't press your nose to the glass and settle for the second-rate produce that the world has to offer. Take a walk in your Father's garden today and eat of His fruit with confidence, knowing that you are His child and therefore His heir, and "no good thing does he withhold from those whose walk is blameless" (Psalm 84:11).

Discovering Your Roots

In case you're still feeling a bit down because of the way we've left things between JD and her father, don't worry. The cliff-hanger may suggest an unsettling scene in which a young girl and her father teeter on the brink of total estrangement, but as we'll see in the next chapter, JD and Jephthah are going to be fine. There is still hope for her relationship with her father because of her relationship with *the* Father.

Maybe you're feeling a little uneasy right now because you can't, with confidence, call God your Father. You want to be a child of God. You want to have a holy inheritance. You've just never been adopted into His family.

It's easy to do. All you have to do is believe in His Son.

Some of you have already done that. You've invited Christ to be Lord of your life, and you've received your holy genes. Are you wearing them? Or are you still walking around in your worldly wardrobe?

As I write this, Father's Day is approaching. Why not make today Father's Day by spending time with your heavenly Father?

Go on. Discover your roots.

Your Genes

1. The cycle that the Israelites repeat in the book of Judges can also describe the cycle that Christians experience in our own spiritual lives. Rebellion. Retribution. Repentance. Rescue. Rest. Which phase of this cycle best describes your current walk with Christ? Why?

2. What do you think about the vow that Jephthah made to the Lord in Judges 11:30–31? Have you ever made a promise to God in a moment of desperation? If so, did you follow through with the promise?

3. Describe a time when someone important to you let you down and fell off the pedestal on which you'd placed him or her. What happened? Did you ever come to see that person in the same way again?

4. Our relationship with our father can sometimes affect our thoughts, opinions, and expectations of God. Think about your relationship, or lack of relationship, with your own father. How does that affect your perception of God?

5. What does 1 John 4:16 say about God? Knowing this, read the "Love Passage," 1 Corinthians 13:4–7, but every time it uses the word *love* replace it with the word *God*. Does this description of God differ from the one you pictured in the previous question? If so, how?

6. Read Romans 8:15–16. Describe the time when you first accepted Christ and received the "Spirit of sonship." Since then, have you consistently turned to God as your *"Abba, Father?"* Why or why not? If you have not yet become one of God's children, what is keeping you from doing so right now?

7. Reread the list of promises mentioned in the section entitled "Tomato Heirs." As a child of God, is there any part of your "holy inheritance" that you are not claiming? Why?

8. *Memorize* 1 John 3:1: "How great is the love the Father has lavished on us, that we should be called children of God! And that is what we are!"

Chapter 5

Her Grace

When he saw her, he tore his clothes and cried, "Oh! My daughter! You have made me miserable and wretched, because I have made a vow to the LORD that I cannot break." "My father," she replied (Judges 11:35–36).

Envelope of Grace

When I was in high school, grace was delivered to me in my mailbox, wrapped in an unassuming manila envelope that sat inconspicuously in a pile of magazines, bills, and junk mail.

Every year the Houston Livestock Show and Rodeo presents a ten-thousand-dollar scholarship to one graduating senior from each of the area high schools. From my high school, I was one of three finalists and was told that there would be a mandatory interview with the scholarship committee before they made their final decision. So when I opened the manila envelope with the familiar Houston Livestock Show and Rodeo logo on the front,

I fully expected it to contain instructions regarding that final interview. Instead, I read the words, "Congratulations on being selected to receive the Houston Livestock Show and Rodeo four-year, $10,000 Metropolitan Scholarship awarded to an outstanding student at Pearland High School."

My heart skipped a beat. My palms started sweating, and I suddenly questioned whether my contacts were working properly or not. Surely I hadn't read that right. What about the final interview? What about the other two finalists who were far more qualified than I to receive such a generous gift? Could it be possible that the committee had actually chosen me to get the scholarship? More importantly, could it be possible that my dream of going to Sam Houston State University was actually going to come true?

I clenched the envelope in my hand and ran back to the house where I charged in the front door. I saw my mom, Sammie, through the kitchen window watering plants in the backyard, so I flung open the back door and began screaming in delight, "I got the Rodeo scholarship! I got the Rodeo scholarship!"

Her jaw dropped with the water hose, and she ran over to sweep me up in a huge hug. "Call up Sam," she said, referring to the college, "and tell them you're coming!"

It's been many years since that afternoon, and I am still humbled by the generosity of those scholarship donors. I didn't deserve that scholarship. I didn't deserve ten thousand dollars for my education. I wasn't any more qualified than the other applicants. But, because of grace—God's grace working through the graciousness of the scholarship donors—I received that awesome gift. Because of grace, I packed up my room the following fall and moved to Huntsville, Texas, to study English at SHSU.

Because of grace, I was the first person in my family to graduate from college.

Because of grace, I was amazed.

An unexpected thing happened over the next four years while I was living off the grace of others. I formed the desire to show grace to someone else. I determined in my heart that someday, after I was out of school and had the financial means, I would be on the other end of a scholarship application. Rather than the one receiving the scholarship, I wanted to be the one giving the scholarship.

I had experienced grace and was forever changed by it. And once I had received grace, I couldn't wait to give it away.

Picture of Grace

While the short story of Jephthah's daughter does not actually record JD receiving God's grace, we can conclude that she did receive grace based on one simple observation: She gave grace away.

When Jephthah sees his daughter running out to greet him and realizes what a twisted turn his tragic vow has taken, the first words out of his mouth are all about him. "Oh! My daughter! You have made me miserable and wretched, because I have made a vow to the Lord that I cannot break" (Judges 11:35).

What? *She* made *him* miserable? How could that be? *He* was the one who made the vow. *He* was the one who couldn't break the vow. All JD did was shake her tambourine.

If you ask me, Jephthah's lament sounds more like Old Testament lingo for, "This is going to hurt me more than it's going to hurt you."

I wonder if JD bought it.

Now, at this point in the story, I am very humbled when I try to picture myself in JD's place. What if I had been the one to receive such awful news? What if it were my life that had been bargained away without my knowledge? What if it were my dreams that were destroyed because someone else decided to use them as collateral?

I can think of a number of ways that I would have responded to Jephthah's grief, and none of them are very nice.

First, I would respond in anger. "You did *what*?" I would scream, and pick up my tambourine only to have something to throw at him.

Then I would attack his character. "How could you be such a hypocrite?" I would yell. "You can save the entire land of Israel, but you can't even save your own daughter? What kind of a hero are you, anyway?"

To be certain, I would negate his feelings and compare them to my own. "Stop crying!" I would demand. "This is *my* life you are ruining here, not yours. How dare you accuse *me* of making you miserable and wretched when *you* are the one who caused this!"

Finally, I would simply rebel. "Well, good luck trying to carry out that promise of yours," I would challenge with a huff. "I don't care what you vowed or to whom you vowed. I will not let you ruin my life like this. I am an independent woman, and I am not yours to give away." Then I would simply walk away and never look back.

Thankfully, that is not how JD responded to her father at all. Rather than lash out at him, she reached out to him. Rather than express her own grief, she acknowledged his grief. Rather than rebel against him, she honored him.

Her father had just done the unthinkable. He had promised her life as a sacrifice. The first words out of her mouth could have been many things, but because of grace, she responded in love, "My father."

In my mind, I picture the scene unfolding like this: Jephthah sees his daughter and immediately drops to the ground in despair. In fashion with Old Testament tradition, he begins tearing his clothes and wailing out in grief over what is taking place. Images of his little girl flash through his mind in pictures as the nightmare unfolds before him. Pictures of JD when she was a baby. Pictures of JD as a little girl, chasing butterflies by day and fireflies by night. Pictures of JD in the garden, picking a handful of flowers and holding them in front of her like a bridal bouquet, giggling as her father watches on. Pictures of JD as a young woman, bravely kissing his cheek goodbye as he goes off to battle.

His cries become so loud that he is inconsolable, and JD realizes that she has never seen her father, the mighty warrior, look so fragile. The severity of the situation sinks in as she deciphers what her father is saying through his tears. Something about a promise? Something about a sacrifice? And at last, she understands.

She is the sacrifice.

Immediately, she runs to her father's side. She gets down on her knees beside him in the dirt so that both hands will be free to hug him. And in a perfect picture of grace, she lets her father, the very man who has betrayed her, cry on her shoulder while she comforts him.

"Oh, Daddy," she whispers, gently stroking his thinning hair. "It's going to be okay."

"I still love you, Daddy."

Recipients of Grace

The simple definition of grace is giving someone something that she doesn't deserve, and in today's culture, it is slowly becoming a foreign concept. When people are victimized, it seems that grace is the *last* thing on their minds. Instead, they want justice. They want revenge. They want answers. They want compensation.

Grace? Well, it might make for a nice baby name, but it's certainly not a practical virtue.

But in this story, we have a woman who thinks differently. A woman who doesn't jump at the chance to play the part of the victim. A woman who gives comfort and love to someone who doesn't deserve it.

Would you have been able to respond with such grace had it been you in JD's shoes?

Chances are, you would respond the same way you did the last time someone got your order wrong at the drive through. Or the last time a friend betrayed your trust. Or the last time a boy broke your heart. If you're like me, you're probably a lot quicker to lash out at someone than you are to reach out to him.

> **The simple definition of grace is giving someone something that she doesn't deserve, and in today's culture, it is slowly becoming a foreign concept.**

Don't feel bad if you're thinking that living in grace does not come naturally to you. That's pretty much the essence of grace, because grace does not come naturally at all.

It comes *super*naturally.

And before we can understand how to give grace, we must first understand the grace that we have received.

Grace is probably one of the most underestimated concepts in the whole Bible. Most Christians think that because they have received salvation, they have received God's grace, when actually, the exact opposite is true. Grace is not a result of salvation; salvation is a result of grace. Because of God's grace, your sins can be forgiven.

> So what does God do? Out of His infinite love for us, He supersizes grace and gives us even *more* than forgiveness.

God's grace is the funnel through which all of His blessings flow. Salvation is simply one of those blessings. Granted, it is a pretty big blessing, but if your focus is on the forgiveness of your sins alone, you're actually missing out on a huge portion of God's grace: His righteousness.

When you accept Jesus Christ into your heart, through grace, your sins are automatically forgiven. That promise is probably what drew you to Christ in the first place. The Holy Spirit convicted you of your sins, you realized you needed a Savior, and you accepted Jesus as Lord of your life.

But here is the awesome thing about grace: it doesn't stop there!

If all grace did was erase your sins, it wouldn't be enough. You'd still be left morally neutral, so to speak. You wouldn't be *un*righteous anymore, but you wouldn't be righteous either. So what does God do? Out of His infinite love for us, He supersizes grace and gives us even *more* than forgiveness.

He gives us the righteousness of Christ.

"God made him who had no sin to be sin for us, so that in him we might become the righteousness of God" (2 Corinthians 5:21). Think of it this way: if your life were a chalkboard, and all of your horrible thoughts, intentions, and actions were written on it, God's grace not only erases the entire chalkboard, it also writes down all of the righteous thoughts, intentions, and actions of Christ on your chalkboard. It's a *full* exchange. Our sin for Christ's righteousness.

Evidence of Grace

When I talk about grace, I sometimes feel like I'm an announcer for a late-night infomercial. "But wait! There's more! Not only do you get God's forgiveness *and* the righteousness of Christ completely free of charge, but walk in God's grace today, and for no extra cost, you'll also receive these fabulous blessings!"

I don't mean to trivialize grace by any means. It's just that any time you think you've received the full extent of God's grace, you realize that there's still even more to come.

But wait! There's more!

One of the other blessings of grace is the ability to endure suffering, and it is here that we really start to get a good look at the evidence of such grace in the life of Jephthah's daughter.

There is no question that JD was about to endure suffering. Her world was rocked the day that she met her father at the door, but rather than crumble under hard times, she squared her shoulders and placed God's grace in between her and her trials.

Paul best describes this blessing of grace in 2 Corinthians 12:9: "My grace is sufficient for you, for my power is made perfect in weakness." No matter what you're going through, God's grace is all you ever need to get through it. After all, our trials are not spotlights on our weaknesses; they are spotlights on God's power!

God's grace was sufficient for Paul when he penned these words almost two thousand years ago. It was sufficient for JD when she faced the biggest trial of her life. And it's sufficient for you, no matter what you're going through today.

Are there times when you've had enough of the single life? God's grace is sufficient.

Are there tears behind your brave face and your empty smile? God's grace is sufficient.

Are you brokenhearted? Disappointed? Frustrated? Lonely? God's grace is more than enough to carry you through this time.

God's grace is so amazing that the weaker we become, the stronger He can make us with His power. The more we hurt, the more His grace can heal our hearts. The more we fall, the more times He gets to carry us.

Once you begin to experience how God's grace gives you the ability to endure suffering, you can, like Paul, *delight* in your hard times. "That is why, for Christ's sake, I delight in weaknesses, in insults, in hardships, in persecutions, in difficulties. For when I am weak, then I am strong" (2 Corinthians 12:10).

Do you delight in your hard times? Do you see your suffering as a chance for God's grace to shine? When you are weak, by the grace of God, you can be strong.

> When we extend grace to others in the things we say to them, we mirror the grace that God has extended to us.

Words of Grace

One of the ways that God's grace has a chance to shine during your times of suffering is through your speech. Whether we want to admit it or not, our words are usually a reflection of what's in our hearts. When we extend grace to others in the things we say to them, we mirror the grace that God has extended to us. However, when our words are less than edifying, it shows just how ugly and dirty our hearts can be.

"The good man brings good things out of the good stored up in his heart, and the evil man brings evil things out of the evil stored up in his heart. For out of the overflow of his heart his mouth speaks" (Luke 6:45).

The old adage "You are what you eat" suddenly seems to need editing: "You are what you *say*."

Sometimes the purest glimpse you can get of a person's heart is in the words she says under extreme pressure. In anger, frustration, disappointment, or fear, the verbal filters are turned off, and the censors stop working. In such times we're often left with slander, profanity, sarcasm, and all kinds of verbal weapons.

You can probably think of something right now that you've said recently that would not be a reflection of God's grace. Colossians 4:6 says, "Let your conversation be always full of grace." Are your conversations full of grace? Are they *always* full of grace?

Consider your latest conversation about your ex-boyfriend. Were your words full of grace when he told you he "just wants to be friends?" What about when you found out about his new girlfriend?

The Bible never claims that our words are easy to control. In fact, it says quite clearly, "No man can tame the tongue . . . With the tongue we praise our Lord and Father, and with it we curse men, who have been made in God's likeness" (James 3:8–9).

Unfortunately, we can bite our tongues until they bleed and still wind up spitting out words that wound others. We just don't have the power to do otherwise.

The only thing powerful enough to tame the tongue is grace.

JD's words of grace were, "My father." In those two words, she reached out to her father and gave him a whole handful of things it would seem he did not deserve. Her love. Her obedience. Her forgiveness. Such gifts you cannot give unless they are wrapped in grace. Such words you cannot say unless they are wrapped in grace.

But in speaking those words of grace under such extreme circumstances, JD gave us a glimpse of the condition of her heart—a heart full of God's grace.

Throne of Grace

The supernatural effects of grace continue to amaze me. I feel as if I could sum up my entire testimony in two words: "by grace."

By grace, I came across the passage of Jephthah's daughter in Judges 11 almost ten years ago. By grace, God comforted me over the years with her story. By grace, I can encourage others with the lessons God has taught me. And by grace, I can write this book for you to read.

God's grace does seem to multiply, doesn't it?

"The LORD is compassionate and gracious, slow to anger, abounding in love" (Psalm 103:8). His grace is such that you can never get enough, and He can never give too much. He never skimps with His grace, and He never plays favorites. There's nothing you can do to earn His grace, and you can never have enough to buy His grace.

"Yet the LORD longs to be gracious to you; he rises to show you compassion" (Isaiah 30:18).

He gives all of it away, and yet He never runs out.

In the last chapter, we mentioned that God, our heavenly Father, does not sit on a pedestal like our earthly fathers, but rather He sits on a throne. It's time now that you start taking a closer look at your Father's throne.

Hebrews 4:16 tells us it is a "throne of grace."

Can you imagine such a thing?

A throne suggests justice and power and ultimate authority. No one else could rightfully sit on such a throne except for Jesus. But instead, He sits on a throne of grace.

The verse continues to say, "Let us then approach the throne of grace with confidence, so that we may receive mercy and find grace to help us in our time of need." Are you in need of God's grace, knowing it is sufficient for your time of need? Do you long for God's grace, knowing it provides what you need to endure suffering? Are you having trouble extending God's grace to others with your words?

Approach the throne. There is enough grace for all of us!

Your Grace

1. Have you ever received something wonderful that you didn't deserve? What was it, and who gave it to you? How did it make you feel?

2. When people do us wrong, many times we lash out at them rather than reach out to them. Can you think of a time when you have monopolized on the opportunity to play the part of the victim? How did the situation turn out? How do you think it would have turned out differently had you responded with grace instead?

3. Read the parable of the unforgiving servant in Matthew 18:21–35. What did the servant receive that he did not deserve? Did the servant do likewise when he had a chance? How did the master respond to the servant's actions?

4. What does this parable teach us about the grace we have received from Christ?

5. When our conversations are not full of grace, sometimes our words become weapons. Read Psalms 55:21; 64:3; and 140:3. Which three weapons do these verses mention? Can you think of a situation when someone used his or her words as weapons against you? How did the words make you feel?

6. How have you used your own words as weapons? Read Psalm 45:2. What should our lips be anointed with? Read Psalm 141:3. Who should control our tongues?

7. When you picture a person sitting on a throne, what images come to your mind? Hebrews 4:16 says that God sits on a throne of grace. How does that differ from the previous image in your mind?

8. *Memorize* 2 Corinthians 5:21: "God made him who had no sin to be sin for us, so that in him we might become the righteousness of God."

Chapter 6

Her Grasp

"You have given your word to the LORD. Do to me just as you promised, now that the LORD has avenged you of your enemies, the Ammonites" (Judges 11:36).

French Toast with a Side of L-O-V-E

My black and white Mary Janes clicked rhythmically on the cement as I rushed from the curb to the back door of my elementary school, eager to begin my day with a mouth-watering breakfast from the cafeteria. (I know, what was I thinking?) The line was never long in the mornings, so I progressed to the cash register quickly, paid my seventy-five cents, and headed to my usual table with the other second graders. Ashley waved; Kim smiled; and Josh did the I'm-too-cool-to-wave head bob. (How do boys learn that so early?)

I was about to sit down in between Josh and Kim when I noticed a folded piece of paper in the chair with my name written on the outside. I picked it up and began to ask, "Who . . ." when Josh diverted his eyes and shook his head ever so slightly, indicating that I should be quiet about the note and not read it until later. Needless to say, that was the longest meal of my life. I thought the school day would never begin, but when the bell for homeroom finally echoed through the hallways, I dashed off towards Mrs. Dillard's classroom, threw my backpack in my tote tray, and slipped into the bathroom to read my note.

In the privacy of the stall, I opened the note with shaky hands. It turned out to be a folded 3 x 5 index card written in pencil with scratchy handwriting, and the note read: "Emily, Emily. E-M-I-L-Y. That's her name. I'll never be the same." Signed: Josh.

It was my very first love letter, and to this day I have yet to receive another that was as sweet or as simple. Josh's words were immediately written on my heart with a permanence that has lasted almost two decades. I must have read that note a hundred times in the days and weeks that followed that special breakfast. I read it to my mom, to my friends. But mostly, I read it to myself. Even long after I had its words memorized and could recite the poem in my sleep, I still felt compelled to open the note, now worn on the edges and slightly yellowed with age, and read it once again.

If It's Written, I'm Smitten

Most of us have a similar message from a boy or a special friend that we remember and clutch tightly in our fists as our hearts well up with emotion each time we read it. Whether you've had your eyes adored or your hair praised or your witty sense of humor acknowledged, you've never forgotten what was said or who said it. We're honored when someone sends us an unexpected card or an encouraging e-mail. A message sent at just the right time can turn a cloudy day into the summer solstice.

We cling to such words because we're flattered that someone has noticed us so intently. Often an admirer or an encourager can notice positive attributes about us that we never would have noticed ourselves. Their words allow us to see ourselves through someone else's eyes, and, as a result, we end up learning something new about ourselves.

I was rummaging in the garage one day when I came across a worn manila envelope amidst the contents of a musty old cardboard box. In it were some miscellaneous (and very cute, I might add) pictures of me when I was young, some random receipts and notes, and a small handwritten notepad that was titled "Emily's 3rd Birthday." In the pages that filled the notebook, my mother had written down every single detail surrounding my third birthday. She described the dress I wore to my party, listed the friends and family members who attended, listed the gifts I received, and even sketched a picture of my very first Superman cake. Because my real mother died when I was ten, I seldom get to relive such memories from my childhood. Reading her words and remembering how much she cared for me made me realize I could still feel her love for me, even though she was no longer physically with me.

The written word can also provide us with comfort. One time, after a tumultuous breakup in junior high, I was curled up in a ball crying on my bed. My eyes were red, my face was puffy, and I had cried myself all the way to the hiccup stage. (You've been there.) Not knowing what else to do, I pulled my lime green

Precious Moments Bible from my nightstand and flipped it open to the middle. Usually this method of "Bible study" is not recommended, but thankfully it worked in this case, for that's when I first discovered Psalm 6:6: "I am worn out from groaning; all night long I flood my bed with weeping and drench my couch with tears."

Jephthah's daughter didn't ignore the significance of God's Word.

My weary body straightened itself at that glimmer of hope. It was as if, even though I couldn't see God, I could still feel His love for me. He had written those words on my heart in order to assure me that I wasn't alone in my sorrow and to remind me that even King David, the man after God's own heart, experienced heartache too.

Her Grasp

It's easy to forget the importance of God's Word sometimes. We tend to think of the Bible as simply this bulky, leather-bound book that makes swishy sounds when we turn the pages, and we forget that it's actually a love letter from His heart to ours. Jephthah's daughter didn't ignore the significance of God's Word. It was written on her heart just like it should be written on ours.

Of course she didn't know the Bible as we know it today simply because the entire canon of Scripture was yet to be written. But she still knew God's Word because she knew His law, as is apparent in the way she responded to her father when he mentioned his tragic vow: "'My father,' she replied, 'you have given your word to the LORD. Do to me just as you promised, now that the LORD has avenged you of your enemies, the Ammonites'" (Judges 11:36).

Why didn't JD argue? Why didn't she reason with her father and disregard his vow as a rash decision mumbled meaninglessly in the desperate trenches of battle? She didn't protest because she knew the law of God.

Among the many laws and guidelines Moses gave to the Israelites, an entire section was recorded regarding the instructions of vows. Today we know those precepts as Numbers 30. "When a man makes a vow to the LORD or takes an oath to obligate himself by a pledge, he must not break his word but must do everything he said" (Numbers 30:2). Neither Jephthah nor his daughter could argue with such a black-and-white command. It is even reemphasized in Deuteronomy 23:23: "Whatever your lips utter you must be sure to do, because you made your vow freely to the LORD your God with your own mouth."

No wonder JD didn't attempt to explain away her father's vow. It was a contract. It was binding. But, I'm convinced that since she was so aware of the finality of the law concerning this statute, she was also probably aware of the rest of the commands concerning vows and therefore saw the irony in her unfortunate circumstances.

If you read further in Numbers 30, you find that if a woman who is still living under her father's roof, as JD was, makes a vow, her father can override it and free her from fulfilling it. For example, picture JD waiting at home, anxious for her father to return safely from battle. After pulling water from the well, she brushes the stray strands of hair away from her face and lifts her eyes to the heavens. With sudden conviction that comes only from the illusion of hopelessness, she raises one fist in the air à la Scarlet O'Hara and cries out, "Oh God! If only you will keep my father safe in battle and deliver him from his enemies, I promise I will commit myself to your service upon his return."

> **If you want to know God and His will for your life, you must strengthen your grasp of Scripture.**

Had JD actually made that vow, the story would end right there. Once her father returned home and heard of her impulsive vow, all he would have to do is simply shake his head and say no. "No, daughter. You're not bound to that rash vow any longer. It's erased."

The exact same vow, yet two different laws apply. JD had to have seen that irony written in the fine print of the Hebrew law, and yet she still obeyed without any hesitation. Why? Because she had a firm grasp of the Lord's message and had His words written on her heart.

Your Grasp

How's your grasp of your Father's message? Do you read His words like you would a love letter, smudging it with your fingers and wiping your fallen tears from the margin? Or does it sit on your nightstand as royalty sits on the throne—never touched and only coming out on special occasions?

Psalm 119:105 says that God's Word is a lamp to our feet and a light for our path, but so many times we seem content just to wander around in the darkness. God wants to give us direction. He wants to show us His will. But we're too lazy to turn on the light!

If you want to know God and His will for your life, you must strengthen your grasp of Scripture. God's Word is a light for your path, and you have to turn on the light!

Searching for North

Often, the hardest part about reading the Bible is knowing where to start. We feel like we have this proverbial compass and we can start walking only once we determine which way is north. We're so scared of walking in the wrong direction or reading the "wrong" thing in the Bible, that we end up keeping our feet planted and our Bibles closed. What if I don't understand? What if I stumble across the "begats" by mistake? What if I miss out on what God wants to say to me because I'm in the Old Testament instead of the New, or vice versa?

There are many helpful tips in Christian circles that can guide you through that directionally impaired feeling, and I'll mention a few of them as we go. But the best advice I can give you is this: Just start reading! Pick a book of the Bible, pick a chapter, and just go for it. The worst thing you can do is not read the wrong thing but rather not read at all. And the wonderful thing about the Bible is that it is *all* inspired by God. He can speak to us through the "begats" just as easily as He can speak to us through John 3:16. Sometimes the words that touch our hearts the most are the ones we find tucked away in the chapters and verses that are seldom highlighted from the pulpit.

Take this book for instance. We've already determined that the story of Jephthah's daughter is not an oft-preached message. I was in college taking an English course entitled "The Bible as Literature" when I read this story for the first time. My boyfriend and fellow English major was in the class with me, and one night we were fulfilling our assignment of reading the entire book of Judges in one sitting. We would take turns reading out loud to each other in order to keep things interesting and entertaining.

It was my turn to read aloud, and I remember breezing through the first half of Judges 11 without emotion or energy. Another judge, another battle—yada, yada, yada—the Israelites get another chance. Then I stumbled across a lady I'd never heard of before: Jephthah's daughter. My reading slowed down, I pulled my Bible closer to my eyes, and I was in shock that I had never heard this story before. What an awesome story for single girls, I thought. Of course, at the time I was sitting next to the man I thought might just be "The One," so I never thought the story would ever affect me directly. But over the years, after that relationship ended, and the next, and the next, I never forgot JD's story or how it became embedded into my heart and my mind. God was planting His Word into my soul in such a way that His message would sprout up precisely when I needed it most.

I guarantee you, if you just start reading, *consistently* reading, God's Word, then He will work out the timing of the message. "Whether you turn to the right or to the left, your ears will hear a voice behind you, saying, 'This is the way; walk in it'" (Isaiah 30:21).

Mapping the Course

That being said, some of you still want some direction. You still want someone to tell you in what order to read those sixty-six books. So here are some tips that might help you.

First, if you've never sought to read the Word, the first thing you should do is develop the habit of reading. A great way to do this is by reading a chapter in Proverbs every day for a month. The book has thirty-one chapters, each short but full of wisdom, and can easily be conquered in one sitting. Not only is this book replete with nuggets of truth you can apply to your everyday life, it also ends with one of the most famous passages for women: Proverbs 31—The Wife of Noble Character.

Once the habit of reading has kicked in, there are many forks in the road that you can choose to follow. If you're a new Christian, the book of John provides a great foundation for your new faith. If you're feeling nostalgic for the Vacation Bible School stories of your childhood, Genesis and Exodus will fulfill that longing. If you need quick energy for daily living, *Go Eat PopCorn* (Galatians, Ephesians, Philippians, Colossians) and read some of Paul's letters. And if you're going through a hard or troubling time in your life, Psalms will comfort you.

While the truth remains that there is no "right" way to read the Bible, you can choose to follow courses that are already mapped out for you if you wish. One-year Bibles offer plans for reading through the Bible in one year, usually by mixing a passage from both testaments in each daily reading. Chronological Bibles present the Word historically rather than in the order of the canon of Scripture. And many Bibles offer a selection of reading schedules in the back along with the glossary and index.

If you are still lost and searching for north, there are many books and Internet sites that can provide more guidelines. One caution about such resources though: While it's good to read Christian books about such subjects as how to read the Bible, remember that your ultimate goal is to actually read the Bible; not to read *about* reading it. Tap into one or two sources, pick a path, and then start reading.

Keeping the Pace

One important thing to keep in mind when tackling this challenging, yet highly rewarding, task is that you must pace yourself and set realistic goals. If you are not a "reader," don't schedule an hour of nonstop reading every night. You will only get frustrated and burned out. If you're a night person, don't try to force yourself into waking up an hour earlier than usual to read your Bible if it ends up making you tired and cranky for the rest of the day. Set aside your lunch hour or some time after dinner to read instead. You know better than anyone else what will work best for you.

One man I knew had a job that required him to work long, hard hours for three or four days in a row. However, those times were always followed by three or four days off. Because a daily reading schedule was impractical for him, he followed a weekly agenda that took into account his random work schedule.

Likewise, don't over-exert yourself to the point that your reading assignments cause other areas of your life to suffer. God does not want us to study so much that we neglect the responsibilities or ministry opportunities He's put in our paths.

It is also important that you allow for hiccups in your reading timetable. Let's face it; sometimes life gets in the way of our good intentions. You might have a deadline sneak up on you at work or a friend's wedding festivities that end up lasting an entire weekend. You need to plan breaks in your schedule to allow for times of catching up, should you need them. As long as you are consistent in your efforts, sometimes the best schedules are the ones that are the most flexible and forgiving.

Documenting the Journey

Just between you and me, I have a quirk when it comes to my Bible. My friends know about it and thankfully love me anyway. Though they tease me and roll their eyes when they think I'm not looking, I'm sure they still find it endearing. The quirk: I can mark passages in my Bible only with a *yellow* highlighter. Green, pink, blue, or even (heaven-forbid) *fluorescent* yellow simply will not do. If it's not plain, boring, sunshine yellow, it will not brush the pages of my cherished B-I-B-L-E.

Because this quirk extends to all my highlighting, including to-do lists, grocery lists, and shopping receipts, I buy yellow highlighters in bulk and stash them everywhere from the glove compartment of my car to the small decorative trunk that sits atop the tank of my toilet. If the need to highlight suddenly strikes, I want to be able to do it *right*.

The first time I read an entire book of the Bible from start to finish, I turned to the front of my Bible and highlighted that book in the table of contents. Though it was one of the smaller books like Jonah or 1 John, I still felt a sense of accomplishment at seeing an *entire* book highlighted. My table of contents became a built-in to-do list as I set upon that task of reading the entire Bible.

You may not be as neurotic as I am about how you mark in your Bible, and some of you may not mark in it at all, believing that doing so tarnishes its worth somehow. But highlighting passages and writing in the margin can become very helpful over time. It makes memorable passages easier to find if the "address" slips your mind, and it helps you track how far you've come when you see some sort of written progress of your efforts.

And for the times when God speaks to you with more words than can fit in the small margins, journaling your thoughts and reactions to His Word can be a priceless habit to develop.

Memorizing Scripture is not an easy endeavor by any means, but it is a necessary endeavor nonetheless.

Journaling can be like writing a letter back to God, thanking Him for the ways in which He spoke to you and explaining how a specific verse really helped you understand a particular situation that you're going through. Sometimes, seeing how a passage pertains to our lives on paper can better help us apply the biblical principles when the time comes.

Sharing the Experience

And now I'll admit I am speaking from a soapbox when I mention the last step in becoming intimate with the Word of God—Scripture memory. For the growing Christian, this is not an option. It is a command. And sadly, it is a forgotten undertaking.

In Psalm 119:11 we are reminded to have God's Word hidden in our hearts. And Joshua 1:8 plainly states: "Do not let this Book of the Law depart from your mouth; meditate on it day and night, so that you may be careful to do everything written in it. Then you will be prosperous and successful."

Many of us do not meditate on God's Word daily, much less have it written on our hearts. We don't know the fruits of the Spirit from the cheeses of France, and we can quote a line from our favorite movie a whole lot easier than we can share a verse with a coworker who is struggling with temptation. Memorizing Scripture is not an easy endeavor by any means, but it is a necessary endeavor nonetheless.

When I led my first small group, I felt very convicted to incorporate Scripture memory into our studies. The girls agreed, and I developed a challenging but doable list of verses that we could memorize together and recite regularly during our meetings. In no time at all I was deemed the "slave driver" as I kept pushing and prompting and encouraging the girls to continue. They teased me that I'd missed my calling to be a schoolteacher and were convinced that we had the hardest small group in the entire church.

My friend Adrienne was especially apprehensive about a multi-verse passage in John. When her time came to recite the verses to us, she maintained the spelling-bee style we had adopted (address, verse, address again) but narrowed her eyes at me during the address portion of her turn as she exaggerated "John 3:16 through a *million!*"

But something amazing happened over those weeks and months of persevering through "Mean Emily's Scripture memory program." Sunday mornings would roll around and we'd be scattered through the rows of the congregation during worship services when the pastor would reference one of the memory verses from the pulpit. Immediately, five heads would bob up from the pew and twist and strain and stretch in an effort to lock eyes with a fellow small group member. "That's one of *our* verses" we'd mouth to each other with girlish grins before settling back into the comfort of our seats sandwiched in between two less fortunate church members who didn't share our special secret.

Though memorizing those verses was hard, it was an integral part of sealing in our lessons. The years have passed and our memories have faded somewhat when we try to recall which books and topics we studied together, but any time one of "our" verses is mentioned in church, we still smile at the secret treasure we share.

Memorizing Scripture gives you ownership of God's Word. It transforms your thinking into His thinking when it's His words that are echoing in your mind and not your own. While some people start memorizing Scripture as a child, it's never too late to begin. And when we consider all of the other useless information that clouds our minds sometimes, there's no excuse not to meditate on His words with such a purpose. Memorizing Scripture means that God can speak directly to you even in those times that you can't have your Bible by your side: while you're driving, in the shower, at the gym. If you do your part in memorizing, He will do His by bringing to mind those valuable verses at the precise time that you need them.

Again, there are many resources that can help you make this a part of your spiritual growth. A great way to get started is to pick up the *Navigators' Topical Memory System* or the *Topical Memory System: Life Issues*, both published by NavPress and available online or at your local Christian bookstore. These packets have tips for memorizing, graphics for those who are visual learners, and handy perforated flashcards that you can carry with you at all times.

Just remember, God did not give us the Bible to scare us or to intimidate us. He gave us His Word in order that through it, we may see Him. His words reveal His character, His promises, and, most importantly, His love. Better than any love note from a secret admirer is a book that replaces secrets with truth. Better than the best romance novel is the story of *unconditional* love. It's a book where the lost get found, the blind can see, good triumphs over evil, and *everyone* gets a second chance. His book is His love letter to us, and it's folded gently and placed in our chairs, waiting for us to discover it and slip away quietly to read it.

Your Grasp

1. Of all of the letters, notes, and e-mails you have received from friends and family, which one has had the most impact on you? Who was it from, and why was it so meaningful?

2. Can you remember a time when a particular Bible verse spoke to you during a difficult situation? What was the verse, and how did it help you?

3. Sometimes we think of the Bible as outdated and not relevant to today's problems. What does Hebrews 4:12 say about the Word of God?

4. Which word below best describes your current Bible-reading habits? Which word best describes what you think your habits *should* be, according to Psalm 1:1–2 and Joshua 1:8?

   Daily   Weekly   Monthly   Sporadically   Never

5. Read Colossians 3:16. Name three things that you will be better equipped to do when you "let the word of Christ dwell in you richly" by memorizing Scripture.

6. Read about the temptation of Christ in Matthew 4:1–11. In verses 4, 7, and 10, how does Jesus respond to each temptation? What does this passage teach you about the importance of Scripture memory?

7. Have you been memorizing the verses at the end of each chapter in this book? If not, make an effort to incorporate this Scripture memory plan into your study as you continue reading. Pray that God will give you understanding and recollection of the verses. If you are in a group, promise to encourage each other and to hold each other accountable in this endeavor. You can do it!

8. *Memorize* Psalm 119:11: "I have hidden your word in my heart that I might not sin against you."

Chapter 7

Her God

"But grant me this one request," she said. "Give me two months to roam the hills and weep with my friends, because I will never marry." "You may go," he said. And he let her go for two months (Judges 11:37–38).

View from the Top

I groaned at the sound of the alarm clock ringing in my ears and flung my hand to the nightstand in search of the cherished snooze button. The oversized red numbers glowed in the darkness announcing the ridiculously early time of 5:15 a.m. *This is crazy!* I thought as I tried to hide from the morning by pulling the overstuffed down comforter over my head. *God never intended for us to get up this early!*

I had just snuggled back into a perfect sleep position when a soft tap on the door interrupted my return trip to slumber land. The door slowly creaked open, and I heard my friend Stacy whisper, "Em, are you up yet?" I moaned an incomprehensible reply and turned my back to the door. "Hurry up and get ready," she whispered again. "We don't have much time. Meet me in the kitchen in five minutes."

And then she did what every non-morning person loathes—she flipped on the light switch, ruining my perfect ambiance of nocturnal bliss—and wisely shut the door behind her before I had a chance to protest. Reluctantly, I rolled out of bed in a mental fog and tried to recall the incentives for this unnecessary rendezvous with the predawn hour. *Ah yes*, I finally remembered. *The sunrise.*

It was spring break of my sophomore year in college, and I had accompanied Stacy and her family to the beautiful city of Boulder, Colorado. That particular morning, we were staying with some friends in their wonderfully quaint and secluded house nestled high on the side of a mountain.

Upon planning the trip the month prior to our getaway, Stacy had mentioned that this house was one of the best places to witness a sunrise, and she almost had me arrested for nature crimes when I admitted that I'd never seen *any* sunrise before, from a mountain or anywhere else. (It comes with the territory of not being a morning person. If God scheduled a sunrise for, say, 10 a.m., I'm sure I would have witnessed many more in my lifetime of mornings.)

I fumbled for my clothes, putting on multiple layers on top of my pajamas, and traded my slippers for hiking boots. When every accessory was finally in place, I shuffled to the kitchen where Stacy greeted me with a smile and a thermos of fresh coffee.

We faced the cold and climbed up the side of a large rock formation that shadowed the side of the house. There we sat, surrounded by snow and silence, in anticipation of the first glimpse of the rising sun. The morning appeared calm and peaceful from our mountainous vantage point, as if the tedious trials of everyday life were dimmed in the shadows and the problems that threatened yesterday had shrunk to a size so small that they had all but disappeared. Though it was still dark in the western parts behind us, I could see that brighter times were on their way as the shadows retreated, inch-by-inch, across the valley.

After about twenty minutes of this heavenly perspective, the sun at last peaked over the horizon. An audible, "Wow," escaped my lips as Stacy simply shook her head and whispered, "There's just something about the mountains, isn't there?"

To the Mountains

"Let me alone two months, that I may go to the mountains and weep" (Judges 11:37 NASB). What is it about the mountains that make them so enticing? Is it the change of scenery? The challenge of the climb? The view from the top? Some people devote their whole lives to mountain climbing and exploration; Jephthah's daughter simply asked for two months.

There must be something special, maybe even supernatural, about the mountains for her to choose that location above all the others to be her refuge during her period of mourning. But what had such a pull on her that she would rather go to the mountains than spend those two precious months in the comforts of her home? It probably wasn't a craving for fresh air, considering the pre-pollution time in which she lived. And it probably wasn't the desire to "rough it," seeing as how everyday conditions were pretty rough already.

But there was *something*. Something about the mountains drew her in. And perhaps by exploring the specifics of her sixty-day radical sabbatical, we'll be drawn to the mountains as well.

Mountaintop Experiences

The concept of retreating to the mountains is not an experience reserved for JD alone. The Bible is full of instances in which people escaped to the mountains for one reason or another. Abraham worshiped in the mountains. Moses received the Ten Commandments on a mountain. David mentioned the mountains repeatedly in his poetic psalms. And even Jesus Himself is noted for retreating to the mountains many times during His ministry. For these men, the mountains were more than an escape. They were a place to pray, a place to praise, and a place to meet with God.

When JD's life was crumbling around her as the news of her father's tragic vow sunk in, the *something* that drew her to the sanctuary of the mountains was more than just the need to escape. She went to the mountains because she wanted to meet with her God.

One of the greatest things we can learn from our wonderful feminine mentor is the intrinsic value of meeting with God. The mountains are where God dwells, and running to the mountains is like running to the arms of our Father. Of course, there's no need to dust off our hiking boots and canteens in order to have our own experience in the mountains. We need only to open our eyes to the One who draws us there. To the One who *made* the mountains.

Place of Privacy

The mountains provide a place of isolation, a place separate and private from the pressures of daily living. In the mountains you are free from sudden interruptions, distracting noises, and unwelcome guests.

There are no cell phones in the mountains. No e-mail. No televisions.

Just you, and silence, and God.

While it's clear that JD spent her two months in the mountains weeping with her girlfriends, I believe that part of that time was spent in isolation as well. Maybe she wandered away from the girls and found a shady spot under a tree to sit and think for a while. Perhaps she wore a path into the ground as she paced the same route over and over again. Or maybe multiple nights went by that she found herself lying on her back, counting the stars, and contemplating the God who created them.

She couldn't spend those two months at home because the need to get away was very real. She needed the isolation that the mountains had to offer. She needed to withdraw from her everyday surroundings.

Even Jesus felt the need to withdraw every now and then, going to the mountains regularly to do so. Sometimes He'd go alone; other times He'd bring His disciples with Him. But no matter how busy or hectic His ministry became, Jesus regularly slipped away to go to the mountains. Sandwiched in between two famous moments in Jesus' ministry—the feeding of the five thousand and Jesus walking on water—is the simple statement that "Jesus . . . withdrew again to a mountain by himself" (John 6:15). These mountainside encounters could easily get buried in the hustle and bustle of the Gospels, but if you read carefully, you'll see just how many of Jesus' private and intimate moments occur in the mountains.

Being single, you may think that you experience plenty of private and isolated moments without a husband or children around to demand your attention. Maybe you live by yourself and are going stir-crazy because your only problem is having *too much* time alone. But understand that even people who live alone seldom experience *quality* isolation. Radios and morning talk shows invade our quiet mornings. The drive to work is tainted with honking horns and blaring music. And we fall asleep to the sounds of canned laughter echoing in syndication from our televisions.

There is a big difference between distracted silence and focused silence. Jephthah's daughter did not retreat to the mountains to clear her mind; she went to *focus* her mind. Being alone and being still are sometimes not enough. In order to make the most of your mountain moments, you must realize that proximity to people is not the issue. The issue is your proximity to God. Having a true mountaintop experience does not involve your being alone with your thoughts; it involves your being alone with *His* thoughts. For it's in the silence that God sometimes speaks the loudest.

Place of God's Presence

The prophet Elijah received one of the most exciting commands in the Old Testament. The Lord told him, "Go out and stand on the mountain in the presence of the LORD, for the LORD is about to pass by" (1 Kings 19:11). What would you do if you received a command like that? Would you go? I know I would!

What if you had a hot date scheduled with the man of your dreams at the same time, and suddenly you had the choice to either go out with a dreamy man or witness one of God's rare physical cameos in this world. I'm convinced that every single one of us would sprint to the side of that mountain and leave Mr. Wonderful behind for a chance to see our Lord. No person is worth missing out on an opportunity like that.

The point here is not to say that a Friday night out on the town with a great guy is wrong compared to a night at home with your Bible. That's not it at all. The point is simply to stress the importance of God's presence in our lives. The absence of God is weightier than any void this temporal world can fulfill.

Elijah followed God's command and went to the mountains to wait for God to appear. He waited through a violent wind that blew dirt in his eyes and shattered rocks into pieces. But the Lord was not in the wind. He waited as the earth quaked fiercely beneath him, knocking him off his feet and onto his knees. But the Lord was not in the earthquake. Then came a fire, heating up the air like a furnace and making his eyes water from all the smoke. But again, the Lord was not in the fire.

At last, after waiting through the mercurial winds, the unsteady earth, and the blazing fire, Elijah heard a gentle whisper. You guessed it; it was the whisper of the Lord.

The Lord promises us that if we go to the mountains, He will appear. The mountains are His dwelling place, and it is there that He reveals Himself to us. "Send forth your light and your truth, let them guide me; let them bring me to your holy mountain, to the place where you dwell" (Psalm 43:3).

Elijah had to muddle through trying circumstances before

God appeared to him on that mountain. Wind, fire, earth-quakes. Such conditions would send most of us running, think-ing that the unfavorable circumstances were proof of God's absence rather than His imminent arrival. But God always shows up when He says He's going to.

We must run to the mountains, confident that the Lord will meet us there just as He promises.

Jephthah's daughter had to face trying circumstanc-es as well before she made it to the presence of the Lord. The winds blew as the shock of her father's vow hit her like a blast of icy, numbing air. But she set her mind on the mountains and determined in her heart to lay that shock at her Father's feet. The earth shook beneath her as the weight of the news sunk in and her legs grew weak and unsteady. But she walked on wobbly legs anyway, step by shaky step, to meet her Lord at the mountains. And finally, as the heat crept up her face from the cauldron of emotions brewing inside of her, she overcame the rising tem-peratures and sought the refreshing breeze of her Lord's gentle whisper.

We must do the same. We must run to the mountains, confi-dent that the Lord will meet us there just as He promises.

Place of Prayer

After we draw away from the crowds (privacy) and rush to-wards the mountains (God's presence), what do we do once we get there? Is our part over? Have we done all we need to do by simply getting out of the world's rain and under the Lord's um-brella? How can we be sure that our time in the mountains is *quality* time and not just grains of sand dripping through the proverbial hourglass?

The answer is simple. We must pray.

In order for a relationship to grow, communication is essential. It's funny how we girls are so quick to notice lack of communication from men but so blind to see it in our own relationships with the Lord.

How many times have you cried out in frustration because a boy wouldn't tell you what he was thinking? *Does he like me? Why won't he commit? Where is this relationship going? Why can't he see that he hurt me?* If we've lived mere minutes as a woman, we've experienced communication aggravation. We know what it's like to long for someone to share his thoughts with us.

Imagine how much more the Lord wants to hear *our* thoughts. The thoughts of His children. The thoughts of His creations.

In one action-packed day recorded in the Gospels, Jesus tried to go to the mountains to pray. Earlier that day, He learned that King Herod beheaded His cherished friend and relative, John the Baptist. Upon hearing the news, Jesus immediately tried to slip away in order to find a place to pray to His Father, but the crowds followed Him. He allowed the tangent, performing many miracles despite His inner desire to be praying in the mountains. But finally, after sending His disciples ahead of Him and dismissing the well-fed crowd, He made it to the mountainside to pray. He didn't let His responsibilities or unexpected circumstances stop Him from finally making it to the mountains. And when He got there, He remained until evening, talking to His Father and sharing His heart in faithful prayer.

How many times do we get distracted on our way to pray in the mountains? We intend to set aside that precious time of prayer, but something suddenly comes up and we're stifled by an unexpected delay. Jesus' time of prayer was postponed by His responsibilities just as ours sometimes are, but He didn't let that stop Him. He allowed brief tangents that were necessary for His ministry, but He *never* ignored an unfulfilled desire to pray.

It's been said that prayer is the most powerful yet the least practiced Christian discipline. For some reason, it's always our last resort. Do you think that prayer was JD's last resort after the news of her father's vow sunk in? I doubt it. For some reason, when I close my eyes and picture her running barefoot to the mountains that day, I can't imagine her *not* praying.

Place of Praise

Coupled with prayer in our mountaintop agendas is the equally important need for praise. "Exalt the LORD our God and worship at his holy mountain, for the LORD our God is holy" (Psalm 99:9). While prayer is the time we spend sharing our thoughts and desires with God, praise is the time we spend exalting God and declaring His holiness.

Though God is the same yesterday, today, and forever, He is so big and so multifaceted that He can appear to us new every morning. On the days when our hearts are broken and our tears blur our vision, God is our *Abba* Father, our Daddy, who wraps us up in His arms and lets us cry on His shoulder. When we trip over temptation and land in the pits of sin, God is mercy as He extends to us a hand of grace. He is our provider, our comforter, our healer, our protector, and so much more. He is our *everything!*

We worship God and praise Him simply by acknowledging

who He is. In that way, He makes it remarkably easy for us to worship Him because He is so wonderful!

Granted, there are times when we're mad at God. We're frustrated that He hasn't given us our deepest desires—a husband, children, a home—and through our anger it's not quite as easy to worship Him. But the truth remains that God's holiness is not dependent upon our happiness. And He is worthy of our worship because of who He is, not because of what He has or hasn't done yet.

Jephthah's daughter had plenty of excuses not to worship God. A broken heart. Broken dreams. Broken spirit. But despite her crummy circumstances, I'm sure that she brought her tambourine—her instrument of praise—with her to the mountains anyway. It's easy to worship and praise and sing to God when all is going according to our master plan. But genuine worship is not convenient worship. It's constant worship.

Place of Provision

The rewards of going to the mountains begin when we start to see the provisional hand of God on our lives. When Abraham, with a heavy heart and heavy steps, trekked up the side of a mountain with his son Isaac beside him, their purpose for the journey was no secret. They were on their way to worship God through sacrifice. However, it was the object of the sacrifice that was unknown to young Isaac as he looked up at his dad and asked innocently, "I see the fire and the wood, but where is the lamb for the burnt offering?" Faithful Abraham responded simply, "God will provide."

Indeed God did provide. On the side of that mountain, just

seconds before Abraham's knife was to pierce the skin of his son, an angel of the Lord stopped him. Abraham's faithfulness was evident, and he looked up to find a ram, caught by the horns, which he sacrificed instead of Isaac. "So Abraham called that place The LORD Will Provide. And to this day it is said, 'On the mountain of the LORD it will be provided'" (Genesis 22:14).

That is a line of truth we should all voice regularly as we seek to meet God in the mountains. *On the mountain of the Lord it will be provided.*

There are a few things that we must understand about the Lord's provisions. For starters, provisions are not the same as blessings.

When the Lord provides, it means that He meets our needs. And the standard for those provisions is not what *we* think we need, because those "needs" are often blurred by our wants and desires. Rather they are what *God* thinks we need. You may think you "need" a husband. The Urge to Merge may hit you stronger than hunger pains at times, but be confident that God knows what we really need better than we do.

The second thing to learn about God's provisions is that they cannot be rushed.

I'm sure Abraham would have really appreciated it if God had stopped him in his tracks at the *bottom* of the mountain rather than at the top. Before he tied his son to the altar. Before his fingers gripped the handle of the cold knife that was set aside to do the unthinkable. But God did not provide the ram for them *until they needed it.*

I've heard it said before that while God is never late, He sure has missed a few opportune times to be early! But that's the awesome thing about God. He is never early, and He is never late.

He is always, miraculously, *right on time.* And He will meet our needs according to *His* perfect schedule, not our tainted ones.

And lastly, God's provisions are not our security. Our security lies in the Provider, not in the provisions themselves.

When the Israelites were wandering in the desert, the Lord provided manna for them to eat. Every morning they woke up and found a day's supply of manna waiting for them outside. Those who tried to gather more than a day's share found it would spoil and rot. They could not store up their food for days to come because the Lord wanted to teach them to rely on Him, the Provider, and not on the manna itself, the provision.

Going to the mountains regularly will allow us to experience God's provisions firsthand. You may look ahead to another two, five, or ten years of being single and think that you don't have what it takes to make it. And you're right. You *don't* have what it takes to make it through another summer filled with couples showers and June weddings. But you *do* have what it takes to make it through today, because that's how God provides. He provides *what* we need *when* we need it and *as* we need it.

On the mountain of the Lord it *will* be provided.

Place of Perspective

Another thing I've noticed in my travels is that it's not just mountains that people want to climb. There is always a race to get to the top of *something.* To the top of the mountains in Colorado. To the top of a volcano in Hawaii. To the top of the Empire State Building in New York City. What makes us use our money, our moments, and our muscles to climb to such heights?

My guess: It's all about *perspective.* If you've ever looked out over the city from the top floor of a skyscraper, you know what I'm talking about. The city looks like you've never seen it before. Smaller. More manageable. Like you could pick up the neighboring buildings and squish them with your fingers.

Whenever you're at the top of something—a mountain, a skyscraper, a roller coaster, whatever—something amazing happens. Your vision . . . *changes*. Suddenly, you can see further than you ever could before. You can see things more clearly. You can see how things fit together. The details of what you're looking at have not changed, but your opinion of them has because you can finally see the big picture.

> When God calls us to the mountains, it's because He wants us to see things from *His* point of view, and God always sees the big picture.

When God calls us to the mountains, it's because He wants us to see things from *His* point of view, and God always sees the big picture. He sees the forest when all we see are trees. He sees the city when all we see is traffic.

He sees eternity when all we see is today.

There is nothing magical about meeting God at the mountains. The events leading up to our circumstances don't undo themselves. The people who've wronged us don't disappear. The outcome of our situation doesn't change. However, when we meet God at the mountains, something miraculous does happen. Suddenly, we're no longer blinded by the details of our everyday problems. The fog lifts and the horizon stretches and gradually we begin to see things from God's perspective rather than our own. Little by little, the big picture slowly comes into focus, and our eyes adjust to discover a world and a plan that is greater than we could have ever imagined.

Finding Mountains in the Plains

Does all of this mean that we have to call up our travel agent this very moment and book a trip to the Swiss Alps in order to meet God at the mountains? Of course not. (Although if you do book that trip and need a companion . . .) It simply means we have to find our mountains in the plains.

"Going to the mountains" simply means that you find a place where you can withdraw from others (*privacy*) and focus on God (His *presence*). Once you are there, spend time in *prayer* and *praise*, and in return, God will *provide* and will help you see things from His *perspective*.

In my life I've had many different "mountains." The first was my bedroom closet when I was in high school. Even though it was way too small to hold everything, I still shoved all of my clothes to one side of the rod and wedged a small white stool in the empty corner. Then I'd escape to my "mountain" with my Bible in one hand and a flashlight in the other and spend time with God while hidden behind my clothes and shoes. This set-up worked well for me for quite some time, and the only distraction was the recurring thought that perhaps I was on the threshold of Narnia after all.

In college I had to try a little harder to find my "mountain." Sometimes it was the fourth-floor study room in my dorm. Or a small cubical in the basement of the library. Other times it was the swing set at the elementary school park. Or the corner booth at Denny's at two a.m.

Over the years, my "mountains" have included everything from my car, my shower, and my office at work to the window seat on an airplane and the sidewalk during morning jogs.

Do you have a mountain that you can run to when you want to meet with God? If so, when was the last time you went to the mountains? Do you go to the mountains immediately at the first sign of God calling? Or do you get there only after you've exhausted all other destinations?

When Jephthah's daughter was troubled, her initial response was to run to the mountains to meet with her God. Is your heart troubled? Are you depressed? Angry? Disappointed? Tired?

Go to the mountains. Your God is waiting.

Your God

1. Think back to a time when you were at the top of something—a mountain, a roller coaster, a skyscraper, or anything else. What was your motivation for getting to the top, and what did you experience once you got there? Describe the view from the top as well.

2. When life isn't going exactly the way we wish it would, sometimes we have great intentions of going to the mountains and meeting with God but end up taking a few detours along the way. What are some other stops you tend to make before you get to the mountains? Name your top three:

The gym   *A good workout always makes me feel better.*

My parents' house   *Mom and Dad could always make things better when I was little; now is no different.*

The mall   *Because sometimes I deserve a little "retail therapy."*

The bookstore   *No matter what my problem, there's almost always an expert who's written a self-help book on the subject.*

A friend's house	*My friends really understand me, and they're always there for me when I just need to talk things out.*
Church	*I may not feel close to God, but at least at church I can look like I'm close to Him.*
The TV	*It's a refreshing change when all of life's problems can be solved in only sixty minutes.*
Work	*After a few late nights at the office, my personal life seems a little more manageable.*
The grocery store	*There's nothing that a little cookie dough won't cure.*

3. Having a true mountaintop experience does not involve your being alone with your thoughts; it involves your being alone with God's thoughts. Read the following verses: Psalm 55:2; Psalm 92:5; Psalm 94:11; Psalm 139:17–18; Isaiah 55:8–9; and Matthew 15:19. What do you notice about the difference between man's thoughts and God's thoughts? Why might these differences be important to remember when spending time in prayer?

4. Read Jeremiah 29:11–13. What promise does God give us in verse 13? What is the condition of the promise? When

you go to spend time with God in the mountains, are there pieces of your heart that you sometimes leave behind? If so, what are they?

5. Think of a time when you really noticed God's provisions in your life. What was the need? How did He provide? According to Philippians 4:19, how many of your needs does God promise to meet?

6. Which of the following appeals to you the most about meeting with God in the mountains, and why?

    The **privacy** of withdrawing from everyday life.
    Being in God's **presence**.
    Having a focusing time of **prayer**.
    The opportunity to **praise** God.
    Experiencing God's **provisions**.
    Seeing things from God's **perspective**.

7. Your God is waiting for you to meet Him at the mountains. Think of a place that you can go right now to be alone with Him. Go there—to your very own mountain—and spend some time in prayer and praise with God. Read Psalm 63 to begin your prayer and Psalm 66 to begin praising Him. (If you are in a group, take turns reading these passages aloud).

8. *Memorize* Psalm 43:3: "Send forth your light and your truth, let them guide me; let them bring me to your holy mountain, to the place where you dwell."

Chapter 8

Her Girls

She and the girls went into the hills . . . (Judges 11:38).

My Girls

The pier was still damp from an early evening shower, but it didn't keep my friends and me from lying on our backs, stargazing in silence.

"We've been through a lot over the past four years," Jennifer said, finally giving voice to the thoughts that had been in all of our heads all day. "Remember the day we all became friends?"

We laughed, each seeing our own version of the story unfold in the patterns of the stars above.

"It was at the Freshman Leadership Retreat," Robin said, "and we were exhausted from spending the entire morning on that dumb ropes course."

"Remember how scary that zip line was?" Jennifer asked.

"No way," Sarah countered. "The zip line was the best part!"

"Anyway, everyone went to the pool to cool off, and somehow we all ended up sitting on the lifeguard stand instead of swimming."

Jen laughed. "I still have no idea how all five of us managed to fit on that tiny platform."

"Does anyone even remember what we talked about that day?" I asked, the hazy memories flooding my mind with equal amounts of humor and nostalgia. My question hovered in the air unanswered.

"I have no idea," Jen finally answered. "The only thing I remember for sure is that when we climbed up that lifeguard stand, we were strangers. But by the time we climbed back down . . ."

"We were friends," I finished.

"Exactly."

I sat up and studied the faces around me: Jen, Robin, Sarah, and Jennifer. In triumph and in tragedy, these were the four girls who formed my family away from my family. Suddenly, I was all too aware that college graduation was around the corner and that this weekend at the lake would be one of our last road trips together. Though I could feel the makings of tears in the corners of my eyes, I blinked them away and shifted emotional gears. "This calls for a Dr Pepper toast!" I exclaimed.

The girls agreed, each sitting up and grabbing a drink from the cooler that still sat in the rocking boat beside the pier. Sarah began, lifting her Dr Pepper can high above her head. "Here's to us—four years and countless cups of coffee later!"

Jennifer, counting on her fingers, added, "Let's see. Six, no seven pets, and several shades of hair color later!"

"To friendship!" Robin cried.

"To friendship!" we echoed.

"May we forever dream each other's dreams," Jen said, "bear each other's burdens, and . . . and . . ."

"And remember each other's maiden names," I concluded as our soda cans clinked together.

And we have.

Her Girls

I often think about the group of girls that JD brought with her to the mountains, and, inevitably, my own group of friends comes to mind. *"She and the girls went into the hills."* Were her girls similar to my girls? Did JD bring her friends with her to the mountains for the same reasons that I brought my friends with me to the lake?

Though different translations of the verse describe the group as her *companions*, her *fellows*, her *friends*, or her *dear girlfriends*, my favorite will always be the description in the New International Version: "She and *the girls*."

When I was in college, that is how my parents always referred to my group of girlfriends. The girls. "Tell the girls that they're welcome to come home with you for Easter." "Have the girls decided on their majors yet?" Even now, many years later, it hasn't changed. "Have you talked to any of the girls lately? Tell them we said hi."

I'll admit, JD's friends are one of my favorite elements of her story. When I read about them, I always get a sudden urge to chat all night on the telephone or look through old photo albums while eating junk food.

In truth, I get the urge for a good old-fashioned slumber party. Bust out the PJ's, the popcorn, and the chick flicks, and let the girl talk begin!

Though there is no doubt JD's circle of friends was very different from my circle of friends (and very different from your circle of friends), I'm also certain that we could find many similarities if the groups were studied side by side. For despite the variables of geography and history, the dynamics of friendship—true friendship—remain constant.

Because JD's story is so abbreviated and her girls are mentioned only a couple of times, I will continue to wonder about them with questions that will never be answered. How many of them were there? What were their names? What were their personalities like? How did they meet? What became of them later?

But such details, if we had them, would probably distract us from the main idea. As it is, JD's girls come into focus just long enough for us to capture a snapshot of true friendship. And by studying what is said and what is not said about them, we'll learn enough to be able to take a look at our own circles of friends.

"She and the girls."

Her girls: the *other* unmarried, unnamed, and unshakable scriptural heroines.

Their History

As a condition of fulfilling her father's vow, JD makes an interesting request. Not only does she want to escape to the mountains to seek refuge in her Father's presence; she also wants to take her girlfriends with her.

No matter how unusual the circumstances, with a request like that, I'd expect a few standard questions to follow from her father. "Who are these girls? How many of you will be going?

Are they the type of girls you can trust with the combination to your luggage?"

But Jephthah didn't barrage JD with a list of questions concerning the company she was keeping. Instead, his response was instinctive. "You may go."

There was no need for Jephthah to ask about the friends that JD wanted to take with her; he already knew whom they were without her ever needing to name them. They were her girls. Her everyday, been-through-it-all, best-friends-forever girls. The ones she laughed with in good times. The ones she cried with in bad.

> Friendship, true biblical friendship, has a supernatural element to it that cannot be ignored.

No, there was no question who JD's girls were. Their history together made them her obvious—no—her *only* choice for comfort and companionship. Even her father could see that. And in a situation as dire as this, only girlfriends of such caliber would suffice.

Friendship of this quality is a rare blessing, indeed. And, as hard as it is to find, sometimes it can be even harder to explain. Some try to stuff friendship into an orderly formula or a systematic three-step plan with guaranteed results and foolproof outcomes. But there is nothing foolproof about friendship. Friendship, true biblical friendship, has a supernatural element to it that cannot be ignored.

In a sense, friendship is an attraction of the soul. The best way I can think of it is that Jesus in me is drawn to Jesus in you. "Magnetism" is how one of my friends describes it.

We cannot study this magnetism, this biblical friendship,

without exploring the Old Testament friendship of David and Jonathan. Though King Saul, Jonathan's own father, labeled David an enemy, the two men developed a relationship that grew stronger than family ties and political persuasions. They had the type of friendship that everyone longs for. A "sworn friendship with each other in the name of the LORD" (1 Samuel 20:42).

While my friend describes it as magnetism, the Bible describes it as being "one in spirit." "Jonathan became one in spirit with David, and he loved him as himself" (1 Samuel 18:1). Perhaps it can be said that the Spirit in Jonathan recognized the Spirit in David, and therefore they were drawn together as friends.

JD, no doubt, had this type of magnetism with the girls she brought with her to the mountains. They had a history. They had built memories. They had poured their hearts out to each other.

When her friends asked her why she wanted to take a sudden trip to the mountains, JD did not have to explain how heartbroken she felt to find out that she would never marry. She simply had to tell them that she found out she would never marry, and without another word, they would automatically know that she was heartbroken.

Their Hands

Aside from knowing that she was heartbroken, her girls would be heartbroken as well, because they too walked around with empty left hands. No wedding rings. No engagement rings. No promise rings. Just naked hands that no man had yet to ask for in marriage.

We know this because the Hebrew word used to refer to JD's friends in this passage is one that is specifically reserved for unmarried, female friendships.

Friendship among maidens.

May we forever dream each other's dreams, bear each other's burdens, and remember each other's maiden names. The toast could have been theirs.

What is the significance that JD's girlfriends were single? It always begins that way, at least. A group of unmarried girls forms a circle of friends until slowly, one by one, they start to marry out of the group.

Perhaps this has happened with you. You used to have single girlfriends. But now they're all married, leaving you to wander around in your newfound position as the proverbial third wheel.

Make no mistake; I'm not suggesting that you need to *sever* friendships due to a change in marital status. But there is a solid argument for *adding to* your circle of friends with some women who are in your similar stage of life. I'm reminded of a cheesy Girl Scout campfire song from long ago. "Make new friends, but keep the old. One is silver and the other gold."

It is quite possible that JD had other friends who she didn't take with her to the mountains. Friends who were married already. Friends whose priorities had shifted because of the bands of gold on their left hands. I'm sure they meant no less to her, but notice who JD turned to when her perpetual virginity was on the line. Her *single* friends. Friends who were in the same stage of life as she. Friends not yet distracted by the demands of a husband and family.

Single girls should have single girlfriends to turn to. This is not a spiritual concept; this is just logical. It is a principle that works for the same reason that married couples should become friends with other married couples. New moms should get to know other new moms. Widows should befriend other widows.

This is the same reason psychiatrists encourage support groups. People need to develop relationships with people who are going through the same thing they're going through. If you're single, this means that you need a close-knit group of single girlfriends.

This very concept led me to one of my most treasured friendships. After college, with all of my best girlfriends living in different cities, I was suffering from extreme friendship withdrawal. Sensitive to my loneliness, my mom, Sammie, called to tell me about Chrissy.

"Carol was telling me about her neighbor's daughter, Chrissy, and I think you need to give her a call," she began. "She's just like you, Emily. She's single, just graduated and moved back to her hometown, and she needs some friends around here. I think you two would have a lot in common."

"So what am I supposed to do?" I asked. "Call this girl and say, 'Hey, you don't know me, but I hear your life is as lonely as mine, so why don't we go grab a cup of coffee?'"

"You don't have to put it like *that*," she replied. "Just invite her to do something."

Reluctantly, I took Chrissy's phone number and debated calling her for a few weeks. I felt silly calling someone out of the blue just because we were both in the same chapter of life, but in the end I figured I had nothing to lose.

We hit it off instantly and quickly discovered we had many similar interests, including a love of musicals. In no time at all, we decided to get season tickets to the theater, and our friendship grew over Sunday matinees in the cheap seats.

A couple of years later, Chrissy married my brother.

What I thought would be just a friendship of convenience between two single girls evolved into a lifelong friendship strengthened by the unexpected bond of becoming sisters.

In an opposite fashion, it took years for my little sister, Meghan, and I to become friends because of the awkward age gap between us. It wasn't until we were older and both going through the same things in life—college, boys, growing up—that we finally clicked. It took us being in the same stage of life for a friendship finally to evolve.

With Chrissy I have a friend who became a sister, and with Meghan I have a sister who became a friend, all because we were sensitive enough to grab onto each other when we both found our left hands were empty.

Their Help

Another aspect that I love about JD's friends is that they were there for her when she needed help.

This is somewhat of an abstract concept, being "there for someone." We often say it but seldom define what it means. "My friends are really there for me when I need them," or "If you ever need anything, I'll be there for you."

Thankfully Scripture spells it out for us a little more clearly. "Carry each other's burdens, and in this way you will fulfill the law of Christ" (Galatians 6:2).

From what we can see in Scripture, that is exactly what JD's friends did. They learned that she had a tremendous burden, possibly the heaviest ever in her young life, and they helped her carry it by going to the mountains with her. When they asked what they could do to help, all JD had to say was, "Two-month slumber party in the mountains," and her girls were ready.

They could have showered JD with empty promises, pat answers, and generic advice on how to survive this hard time, but instead of helping with words, they helped with actions.

When my real mother died, I remember that my Sunday school teachers gave me a Precious Moments figurine. I remember that my aunts cleaned our house. I remember that people brought us food. And I remember that the PTA dedicated some books to the school library in her honor.

But I don't remember a single word anyone said to me.

Ecclesiastes 4:10 says, "If one falls down, his friend can help him up." Notice it does not say, "If one falls down, his friend can *tell* him how to get up."

It can be so hard to figure out what to say to someone when she is going through a difficult time. You can search the Bible for the perfect Scripture verse to pass along to her. You can scour a Christian radio station for a song that might speak to her. Or you can *do* something.

It doesn't even have to be something spectacular or something as time-consuming as a two-month stint in the mountains. It can be as simple as making a cup of coffee.

When I was in college, Jennifer (one of my girls from the beginning of the chapter) was great at this. When one of us was down, probably because of some boy, she would always put on a pot of coffee. Instead of smothering us with words, she made coffee.

Just the other day I got a card in the mail from Jennifer, and in it was a five-dollar Starbucks gift card. The note said, "We may live in different cities, but I can still make you coffee." Even though she lives hours away, she still finds a way to help with actions.

Their Hurt

Considering what we've explored so far about JD's girls—their history, their hands, their help—it naturally follows that when JD hurt, her girls hurt as well. JD clearly expresses her desire to go to the hills to weep *with* her friends. The possibility that JD's were the only tears shed during those eight weeks is simply not feasible.

I remember being in Walt Disney World when I was really young, before the days of cell phones and free long distance, when my mother slipped away to call her best friend, Cheryl, from a phone booth. When she returned, her eyes were puffy, her face was red, and I could tell she'd been crying. When I asked her why, she explained, "Cheryl's sad, honey, so I'm sad too."

We were in the Magic Kingdom! The happiest place on earth! But because her friend was hurting, my mom hurt too.

Most men cannot understand this unique quality that female friendships share—the ability to cry together. But once more, this is where the Old Testament friendship of David and Jonathan proves to be exceptional.

When the time came for these two friends to separate, the Bible says that they cried. Two grown men, both strong and powerful, actually cried together because the time had come for them to go their separate ways. "Then they kissed each other and wept together—but David wept the most" (1 Samuel 20:41).

Their friendship, their "magnetism," was so strong that when one hurt, the other hurt with him.

In these self-centered times in which we live, it is rare to find a friend who will weep with you. When was the last time you went through a breakup and your friend actually cried with you? It typically doesn't happen, does it? More often than not, when you experience heartache, it does nothing but serve as a catalyst for someone else to relive her own heartaches. "You think Rhett broke your heart, Scarlet? Well let me tell you what Neil Bryant did to me in the twelfth grade!"

That's what I love about JD's friends. This trip to the mountains was not about them. For these two months at least, it was all about JD. They didn't try to "one up" her with stories of, "Well at least your father isn't trying to arrange a marriage with someone dreadful like mine is." They didn't try to invalidate JD's feelings by unpacking baggage of their own.

Instead, they hurt because she hurt. The tears they shed were for JD.

Their Honesty

Equally important is that JD's friends were honest with her. They could have pointed fingers, shifted blame, encouraged rebellion, or promised revenge. Instead, as hard as it was, they spoke the truth.

The truth in this situation was that JD's father made a vow that must be carried out. Crying would not change it. Whining would not change it. Arguing would not change it. What was done was done, and to deny it would do nothing more than provide JD with a false sense of happiness.

Unfortunately, our closest friends are sometimes the last ones to be honest with us. Instead of helping with a situation, they will exert all of their energy distracting us with false truths.

JD's friends could have done this quite easily. After all, they had an ample amount of ammunition with which to work: *Your father is a terrible man. This is all his fault. How could the law be so unbending? It's not fair! You should appeal. You'd make a wonderful wife—how could he ruin that for you?*

> Anyone can tell you what you want to hear, but it takes a true friend to tell you the truth even when the truth will hurt.

Such lies and distractions are called kisses from an enemy, and the Bible is quick to warn us against them. "Wounds from a friend can be trusted, but an enemy multiplies kisses" (Proverbs 27:6). Anyone can tell you what you want to hear, but it takes a true friend to tell you the truth even when the truth will hurt.

This can be a hard principle to live by. Sometimes it means risking your entire friendship with someone because you know she will not enjoy hearing the truth. *That boy, the non-Christian that you're dating, is completely wrong for you. No, I don't think you should live with your fiancé before you get married.* As a friend, sometimes it feels like it would be a whole lot easier just to keep your mouth shut.

There are two things that show us that JD's friends did not defraud her during their mega-camp out in the mountains. The first is that they let JD return home. Lesser friends would have staged a coup against Jephthah and hired a lawyer to search for a loophole in the law. JD's friends supported and respected JD's decision to be obedient.

The second is that every year, the girls spent four days honoring JD's actions. Lesser friends would have remembered JD just enough to gossip about her. But these girls, JD's friends, commemorated JD because they were confident that she had done what was right.

Their Happiness

The last nugget of inspiration I gleaned from JD's relationship with her girls is more of a reflection of JD's character than it is of theirs. Granted, the story is short, and the majority of the details are left for us to imagine, but there is no hint of resentment in JD's return to her father.

We've already established that JD's friends were single. That fact naturally leads to the conclusion that they would get married someday. They would find husbands. They would become wives. They would start their own families.

They would all get the life that JD had dreamed of for herself.

Does this sound familiar?

Chances are, you're not reading this book if none of your friends have gotten married yet. You're reading it because you're one of the last ones left to hear those life-changing words, "Will you marry me?" You've walked down the aisle draped in pink satin one too many times, and you're about to scream if you don't get to be the one in white . . . soon!

It's hard to be happy for your friends when they seem to be getting what you've been praying for, isn't it?

With JD, it seems that her friendships were such that she and the girls could be happy for each other, no matter who received the blessings. Her friends remembered her in a positive light: as the girl whose life was a sacrifice to the Lord. Not as the girl who was jealous of all of her married friends.

This can be tough to remember when ten out of twelve Saturdays in the summer are booked with weddings or bridal showers. In seasons like these, the news of another engagement can trigger a clandestine roll of the eyes and a forced smile rather than genuine happiness. I've seen these looks of envy before, and I've been guilty of them myself. But, as JD reminds us, jealousy has no place among friends.

Your Girls

I'm sure you've been evaluating your own friendships as you've read about JD's friendships. It's easy to see the need for improvement when it comes to our friendships with our single girlfriends.

What kind of history do you have with your friends? Do you have the kind of bond that JD had with her friends or that David had with Jonathan? If Jesus in you can see Jesus in them, it's a good place to start.

If all of your friends have gotten married and left you flying solo, I hope you see the benefit of adding to your circle of friends. Whether you're single and eighteen or single and forty, having godly girlfriends—ones who are in the same stage in life as you—is a must.

Join the singles' group at your church. If you don't have a singles' group, you could find a church that does or start your own group. A great place to begin is by starting a small group. You don't have to be a biblical scholar to do this. Just pick a book—this one for example—and invite a group of girls over to your house to discuss it once a week. In no time at all, you will bond over the discussion questions and find yourself searching for more books to study just to keep the group going.

By treating your friends the way you wish to be treated yourself, you will attract the type of friends who will last a lifetime. Be the first to help with actions when everyone else is stumbling over mediocre advice. Show that you genuinely care by empathizing with your friends and hurting when they hurt. Speak with honesty no matter how awkward or difficult the truth is. And if that friend comes to you all of a sudden with a diamond weighing down her left hand, be happy for her. Celebrate the blessings that God has given her and honor your friendship, your magnetism, by not only sharing in her hard times but sharing in her joy as well.

> By treating your friends the way you wish to be treated yourself, you will attract the type of friends who will last a lifetime.

Often times, I wish I could jump into the pages of my Bible and hang out with JD and her friends. Go to the mountains with them. Laugh, cry, and talk with them. Anything to become one of the girls.

And times like now, as corny as it sounds, I wish I could jump out of the pages of this book and get to know you. Go out for coffee. Go shoe shopping. Anything to add you to my circle of friends.

But since that's probably not going to happen even with modern advances, I'll just have to be content with praying for you. Hopefully that will be enough to start a bond that we'll be able to continue on the other side of heaven.

Until then, know that I am praying. For you. For every single one of you reading this book. That God will use His Word to speak to you when the single life gets a little old. That the story of Jephthah's daughter will comfort you the same way it comforts me. And that you'll find and foster awesome godly friends who will be around for a lifetime.

Friends who will bear your burdens, dream your dreams, and remember your maiden name.

Your Girls

1. Have you ever had a friend with whom you've experienced "magnetism"? How did you meet, and why did you become so close? What is your relationship like today?

2. If you had been one of JD's friends, how would you have responded when she told you about her father's vow and her willingness to obey it?

3. How does Proverbs 27:17 reinforce the viewpoint that it is important to have Christian girlfriends who are in the same stage of life as you? Do you currently have friends who fit in this category? Why or why not? What steps might you take to add to your circle of friends who are in your stage of life?

4. Read Proverbs 27:5. Have you ever had to rebuke one of your friends? How did she respond? Has someone ever rebuked you? What was your reaction?

5. According to 1 John 3:14, how are we to show our love to our friends? What are some practical ways that you can show love to your single friends?

6. Read the parable of the workers in the vineyard in Matthew 20:1–16, paying special attention to verse 15. Are you ever envious when the Lord is generous to others? What about

when someone much younger than you gets married? According to 1 Peter 2:1, what are you to do with envy?

7. The following passages are examples of how Paul prayed for his fellow Christian friends: Ephesians 3:16–19; Philippians 1:9–11; and 2 Thessalonians 1:11–12. Do you pray for your friends like Paul prayed for his? Do you pray for your friends at all? Start now by picking one of these passages and praying it over your friend. If you are in a group, take turns praying aloud for each other.

8. *Memorize* Proverbs 17:17: "A friend loves at all times, and a brother is born for adversity."

Chapter 9

Her Grief

. . . and wept because she would never marry (Judges 11:38).

The SUV Caravan

The winter winds were harsh that night. At least that's how I remember it in my mind. Fierce winds. Biting temperatures. Intimidating December weather that threatened even the warmest of Christmas cashmere.

But the truth is I live in Texas, so in hindsight it couldn't have been *that* cold. Maybe forty-five or forty degrees at the least. In reality it definitely was not as cold as I remember feeling.

But perhaps that is because I was actually cold on the inside.

We were on the backside of the winter holidays with all of the presents opened, all of the food eaten, and all of the carols sung, and I was feeling pretty good having made it through one more holiday season *single*. But any time you build up to a climax like

Christmas, you can brace yourself for at least a little bit of melancholy to follow. This year was no different.

My cousins were about to leave town, so my siblings and I wanted to spend one last evening with them without the company of the generations between which we were sandwiched. That meant that the grandparents kept the grandkids, and we, the middle generation, set off for an evening of fajitas and tacos—a relief from the mounds of turkey and dressing that were still falling like manna from my parents' kitchen table.

With so many of us, we each hopped into our own cars and drove to the Mexican restaurant in a caravan. Somehow, I ended up as the caboose, which I didn't mind at all, until we reached a stoplight that gave me enough time to examine all of the cars in front of me.

They were *all* SUVs.

What seemed like an insignificant coincidence at first slowly evolved into more as the details hit me one by one. Everyone in the cars ahead of me was riding with his or her *spouse*. My cousin and his wife. My brother and his wife. My *other* brother and his wife. And my sister and her husband. Not only was I following a long line of family vehicles, I was following a long line of *families*. Husbands. Wives. Mothers. Fathers. Each in their perfect little SUVs with their perfect little families.

And me trailing behind.

In my *sedan*.

Grief blew through the air that December evening and settled on me in my little bronze car. And as hard as I tried, I couldn't stop the tears from squeezing out. I *thought* I had made it through the holidays. I *thought* I was okay. But my tears (and the SUVs) reminded me that I wasn't through grieving after all.

For whatever reason, God had still not blessed me with a husband. And as much as I trusted Him, as much as I believed His will and His timing were perfect, for the moment at least, I had to weep.

Her Grief

The Bible says that JD wept. To me, that is *huge!*

But even more significant than her tears is the reason behind her tears. She cried *because she would never marry.*

That doesn't sound right, does it? JD is our role model. Our scriptural heroine. Heroes don't *cry.* They're supposed to be strong. They're supposed to be impenetrable.

They're supposed to be unshakable.

Yet JD's tears don't seem to reflect the image of an unshakable single woman. At first glance, it appears that we've finally discovered our heroine's kryptonite when, in fact, all we've really done is unveil yet another one of her strengths.

Many would say that if a single girl cries because she isn't (or won't be) married, then she is obviously missing one or more of the following: belief in God, trust in God, faith in God, or patience with God.

I've certainly heard that before. But, more than anything else, I've heard the claim that if I experience grief over being single (or any other trying circumstances), then I must not be . . . *content.*

That sounds so spiritual, doesn't it? *Contentment.*

Now, be honest. When you've heard sermons or read other books about being single, when was the last time anyone ever told you to go ahead and cry about it? I can't remember that ever happening.

Instead, you're told *not* to cry about it. People point to Paul, who told singles that it was best for them to stay unmarried as he was. They point to Ruth, whose strength seemed to shine the brightest when she was single. Or they quote Isaiah 54:5, reminding you that "your Maker is your husband—the Lord Almighty is his name," insinuating that if *that's* not enough for you, then . . .

However, in a category that she seems to have all to herself, there stands Jephthah's daughter, with a message that seems to say that crying over your marital status isn't just acceptable; it's encouraged.

I don't know about you, but I felt a wave of relief sweep over me at this point in JD's story. It was like God Himself was validating every tear that I'd ever shed over the fact I was still single, and I finally felt like I wasn't insulting Him or doubting Him because I grieved from time to time.

Before, I'd somehow gotten the impression that as long as I still felt sad and as long as I still desired deeply to get married, I must have leaps and bounds to grow in my spiritual walk. I must not be "there" yet. I thought I was supposed to strive for some sort of spiritual numbness or apathy, and as long as I still grieved and as long as I still cared, I had not yet reached that spiritual goal.

If you have ever felt that way, then I hope that this chapter encourages you. If you have ever felt shame in your tears, then I hope this chapter gives you freedom. And if you have ever been embarrassed to admit that your heart still longs for a husband someday, then I hope that JD's tears will help you validate your own.

The Grief of Jesus

The shortest verse in the Bible should be our first clue that our tears are not an insult to God. "Jesus wept" (John 11:35.) If Jesus, God in the flesh, experienced and expressed grief when He was physically here on the earth, doesn't it naturally follow that we would experience and express grief as well?

But, you might argue, in this situation Jesus was crying over the death of His friend, Lazarus. He was not crying because He would never get married. Tears shed over death seem much more acceptable than tears shed over unfortunate circumstances.

While this is true, we must remember that Jesus held the power over death in His hands. Before He wept, He told Martha that Lazarus would rise again. After He wept, He called Lazarus out of the grave and restored his life to him. If He knew His friend's death was temporary, why then did He still shed tears?

> If Jesus, God in the flesh, experienced and expressed grief when He was physically here on the earth, doesn't it naturally follow that we would experience and express grief as well?

He cried because He experienced loss. In this case it was the loss of His friend, and even though it was a temporary loss, it was still loss nonetheless.

JD's grief could be boiled down to loss too. The loss of hope. The loss of an expectation. The loss of her heart's deepest desire.

Maybe not the death of a person, but still the death of a dream.

Later Jesus expressed grief once again when He knew that His crucifixion was just hours away. Wanting to go "to the mountains" to meet with God, Jesus led His disciples to the Garden of Gethsemane to pray. Mark 14:33–34 says that He was "deeply distressed and troubled," and that His soul was "overwhelmed with sorrow."

Circumstances were not as Jesus wished. He did not look forward to the physical pain that the cross would cause. In His grief, He prayed three times that God would spare Him from the upcoming events and "take this cup" away from Him.

The cross that you bear may be the ring finger on your left hand. It's not Calvary, of course. It's not even in the same realm as that. But you still want to cry out to God to spare you from the pain and to "take this cup" of singleness from you.

It's okay to pray for that. Jesus understands. He grieved His circumstances with sorrow and emotion just like you. Tears have a place in our Christian walks. Grief is allowed. Sorrow is acceptable. There is "a time to weep and a time to laugh, a time to mourn and a time to dance" (Ecclesiastes 3:4).

I hope that this truth gives you comfort as it did for me. I hope that you are beginning to understand that God *does* care. And I hope that you can see that your tears are important to Him.

That being said, please don't reach for the box of tissues *just* yet . . .

Non-Alcoholic Grief

In looking at Jesus' grief before the cross, we cannot ignore the most telling part of His heartfelt prayer: "Yet not what I will, but what you will" (Mark 14:36).

Jesus' grief ended with His declaration of His acceptance of God's will. He prayed for His grief to be taken away. He prayed for an end to the pain. But above all, He submitted Himself *and* His grief to God's plans.

If only our grief were wrapped so neatly.

Most of the time, our "grief" is not grief at all. We may think it is grief. It may feel like grief. It may look like grief. It may even taste like grief. But the saltiness of our tears can be deceiving, and the aftertaste often proves otherwise.

It is not grief we are pouring out, but whine.

I never recognized this in my own life until someone pointed it out to me. I was rambling on about my life one day, complaining that it was not turning out at all like I had hoped or expected, when my friend got a funny look on his face.

"I feel drunk," he said out of the blue.

Knowing that he had never touched a drop of alcohol to his lips, I was terribly confused. "What do you mean, you feel drunk?" I asked. "Why?"

His answer cut deep. "Because of all the whine you've been giving me!"

That's when I knew I needed to learn the art of "nonalcoholic grief"—grief without whine!

Nonalcoholic grief can be difficult to explain, but there is no better place to begin than by exploring the story of the Israelites' flight from Egypt. Caution: You will most certainly have a hangover after digesting all of the whine poured forth from the lips of this bellyaching group as we look at a few chapters in the book of Exodus.

To set the scene, the Israelites had just witnessed the Lord do amazing things. After ten miraculous plagues that God inflicted upon the Egyptians, Pharaoh's heart finally softened enough that he allowed the Israelites to flee under the direction of Moses.

The journey to the Promised Land had begun at last! The Israelites were free!

However, at the first (notice that it was not the second or the third, but at the *first*) sign of trouble, the whining begins.

At the edge of the Red Sea, the Israelites noticed that Pharaoh's army was pursuing them. Rather than trust the God of promises, they began complaining to Moses. "Was it because there were no graves in Egypt that you brought us to the desert to die? . . . It would have been better for us to serve the Egyptians than to die in the desert!" (Exodus 14:11–12).

You know what happened next. Moses parted the Red Sea, and the Israelites experienced yet another one of God's miracles: They crossed through on dry land. You would think that would be enough for them, but the whine continued to flow.

When they got hungry, the Israelites' complaining continued. "If only we had died by the LORD's hand in Egypt! There we sat around pots of meat and ate all the food we wanted, but you have brought us out into this desert to starve this entire assembly to death" (Exodus 16:3).

The Lord answered by raining down manna from heaven. Another miracle. Another reason for the Israelites to quit whining . . . until they got thirsty, that is.

Again they complained to Moses. "Why did you bring us up out of Egypt to make us and our children and livestock die of thirst?" (Exodus 17:3). This time, God provided water miraculously out of a rock.

Are you feeling the effects of the whine yet?

If we had been on that journey with the Israelites and asked them if they were grieving, they would probably have said yes. They had loss. They had sorrow. They had tears. But notice that not once did they ever reconcile their tears with submission to God's will.

Whining Versus Weeping

There is a significant difference between the tears of Jesus in the Garden of Gethsemane and the tears of the Israelites in the desert.

Jesus grieved, *truly* grieved. The Israelites whined.

It's the difference between real tears and crocodile tears. It's the difference between one-syllable words and one-syllable words that are pronounced as three.

When I studied journalism in high school, we were taught that stories should be "skirt length"—long enough to cover the subject, but short enough to be interesting. I often think that grief is the same way. I've noticed that when my "grief" goes on too long, it often turns to rambling and inevitably culminates into whining.

You've noticed this with little kids. When a little boy is *really* hurt—a scraped knee or a busted lip—he'll usually cry out in pain right away. It is loud and he cries hard, but he usually stops after the initial shock has worn off. However, get that same child in the middle of a candy store and show him all the candy that he can't have, and you'll have tears that last the rest of the night!

Whining also tends to point fingers while weeping does not. Notice that the Israelites always blamed Moses. "It's all your fault!" they repeated time after time.

When we whine, we're no different from the Israelites.

Sometimes we'll blame anyone for the fact that we're still single. Whose fault is it today? Your ex-boyfriend's who wasted two years of your life and still didn't follow through with a ring? Your parents' who got divorced when you were six, leaving you with negative expectations of marriage? Or is it God's, who has the gall to withhold the one thing you *know* would bring you happiness—a husband?

Weeping is okay. Whining, complaining, griping, arguing, or wallowing is not.

Whine also leaks out with envy. So many times we're not grieving *our* situation, because if we were to be honest, our situation is really not that bad. Instead, we're grieving that our situation is not the same as someone else's.

Make no mistake; grieving over your marital status is not a bad thing. When we hurt, God cares. It is the perfect opportunity for Him to comfort us, and He loves to comfort His girls. But examine your tears long before you get puffy eyes and a red nose. Are your tears falling at the feet of Jesus as you look up at Him and say, "It's ultimately not my will that I want, but Yours"? If so, then your tears are pure, and God will comfort you as you grieve. "Blessed are those who mourn, for they will be comforted" (Matthew 5:4). But if your tears are laced with whine, don't expect comfort to come as easily.

The Bible says that Jephthah's daughter *wept* because she would never marry. *Weeping* is okay. Whining, complaining, griping, arguing, or wallowing is not.

The Joy of Grief

Lest you think that there is no real problem with whining versus weeping, we must next discover what happens *after* we grieve. Whining turns into more whining. But grief, well, grief turns into joy, as the Bible promises in many different places:

- Those who sow in tears will reap with songs of joy. He who goes out weeping . . . will return with songs of joy (Psalms 126:5–6).
- Weeping may remain for a night, but rejoicing comes in the morning (Psalm 30:5).
- I tell you the truth, you will weep and mourn while the world rejoices. You will grieve, but your grief will turn to joy . . . Now is your time of grief, but I will see you again and you will rejoice, and no one will take away your joy (John 16:20, 22).

It's easy to confuse joy with happiness. After all, the words are considered synonyms by most. They both have positive connotations. They both suggest a state of euphoria. They both paint a smile on your face. But don't be fooled; they are not the same thing. Joy is so much more than happiness ever could be!

Happiness looks at the here and now, whereas joy has an eternal perspective on life. Happiness gets distracted by current circumstances, but joy sees Christ and *His* plan for the universe and celebrates being a part in it. Happiness pouts when it doesn't understand God's ways. Joy places God's sovereignty above His mystery and rests in His peace.

Happiness focuses on self. Joy focuses on Christ. In fact, I'd venture to say that one couldn't experience joy at all apart from Jesus Christ.

Happiness is superficial and can come and go a hundred times during the day. Happiness can be a result of light traffic during rush hour. A great bargain at the mall. The perfect bite of cheesecake.

But joy—joy is everlasting and is the result of Christ and Christ alone.

If you've ever read Psalms, which is a great book of the Bible for anyone who is grieving, you recognize the sheer nakedness of the emotion as verse after verse bears the soul of the writer. Though it is a book that honestly expresses pain, sorrow, and repentance, more than anything else, it is a book about joy.

The word *joy* appears over fifty times in the book of Psalms, while the word *happiness* does not appear at all.

Likewise, in the book of Deuteronomy, there is a law that says that a new husband should not be sent off to war during the first year of his marriage. Instead, he should be "free to stay at home and bring happiness to the wife he has married" (24:5).

The wording of this law is so significant. The husband can bring *happiness* to his wife. Notice that it doesn't say he can bring *joy* to his wife.

So what does this mean for Jephthah's daughter and for you and for every other single woman who has reconciled the fact that a husband will not bring joy? Should that fact alone take away the grief of being single? And if it doesn't automatically take it away, how can the grief turn into joy?

Again, I turn to the Psalms for an answer to this mystery and focus on Psalm 13, a prayer of David, which shows us a perfect example of grief turning into joy. The first and second verses are full of pain and sorrow: "How long, O LORD? Will you forget me forever? How long will you hide your face from me? How long must I wrestle with my thoughts and every day have sorrow in my heart?"

Those words could have easily come out of my journal. "How long, O Lord? Have You forgotten about me? How long do I have to endure this loneliness and wait before I get married?"

> If you want your grief to turn to joy, shift your attention away from yourself and focus on God.

That sounds like grief to me. Honest, naked, heartfelt grief.

Now, skip down to the last verses in this chapter. "But I trust in your unfailing love; my heart rejoices in your salvation. I will sing to the LORD, for he has been good to me" (vv. 5–6). Those verses sound like joy.

The same chapter. The same prayer. Yet somehow there is a complete transition from grief to joy in six simple verses. What changed?

What changed is the focus of David's prayer. In the first two verses, David focuses on himself. In the last two, he focuses on God. That teaches us a great lesson that I hope you don't easily forget. If you want your grief to turn to joy, shift your attention away from yourself and focus on God.

Something Blue

Being a Christian single does not make you immune to the hurt that can accompany the single life any more than being a Christian parent frees you from the trials of raising a child.

"In this world you will have trouble." Jesus Himself made that promise in John 16:33. Those who try to tell you otherwise are either lying to you or lying to themselves.

But again, shift your focus to the second part of Jesus' promise, and the joy begins to surface. "But take heart! I have overcome the world!"

If the desire to be married is real and strong within you, then you will probably continue to get the blues from time to time no matter how strong your walk with Christ is. Take those blues to Christ. Lay them at the foot of the cross and see how God sends joy in your life.

Try praying like King David prayed in the Psalms. To keep from getting distracted, it can be very helpful to write out your prayer in a journal. Start by pouring your heart out to Him as openly and honestly as you can. Tell Him where you hurt. Tell Him why you hurt. If you're disappointed, tell Him that. If you're tired of waiting, let Him know. Don't hold anything back; just wring your heart out like a sponge until there is nothing left.

Then shift your focus. Turn your prayer away from yourself and onto Him. Thank Him for the blessings in your life. Tell Him what He means to you. Praise Him for who He is. Focus on salvation. Focus on the cross. Focus on Christ's righteousness and marvel at His holiness.

In time, your grief will turn to joy, and by turning your focus to God, you will be able to end your prayer with the words of Jesus and mean them: "Yet not what I will, but what You will."

Your Grief

1. Can you think of a time when you shed a few tears over not being married yet? If so, what sparked your grief? Were you ever able to reconcile your grief with God's sovereignty, or are you still working towards that?

2. Do you agree with JD's desire to grieve her marital status? Why or why not? How might the story have turned out differently if JD had whined instead of wept?

3. Read God's response to the Israelites' whining in Numbers 14:26–30. What did their complaining ultimately cause them to lose? When you talk to God about your marital status, are you really grieving, or are there times when you are whining instead? How do you think God feels when His children whine and complain against Him?

4. Read Psalms 42 and 43, focusing on the following stanza that is repeated three times:

   Why are you downcast, O my soul?
   Why so disturbed within me?
   Put your hope in God,
   for I will yet praise him,
   my Savior and my God.

The writer seems to have head knowledge of the hope that comes from God, but who or what still needs convincing? Have you ever felt the same way? When?

5. Read about the sinful woman who anointed Jesus with perfume in Luke 7:36–50. Where did she let her tears fall? How did Jesus respond to her tears? Do you think her tears were turned to joy? If so, why?

6. In Revelation 21:1–4, what does God say He will do with our tears? What else does He promise in verse 4?

7. According to 2 Corinthians 1:3–4, what are we to do when God comforts us? How might you carry out that mission?

8. *Memorize* Psalm 30:5: "Weeping may remain for a night, but rejoicing comes in the morning."

Chapter 10

Her Guarantee

After the two months, she returned to her father and he did to her as he had vowed (Judges 11:39).

The Laugh after the Sorrow

Something strange and unexpected happened during my mother's funeral.

I laughed.

It didn't happen during the service, of course, but afterwards, when all of our friends and family gathered at our house for the traditional post-graveside potluck dinner. At ten years old, I was experiencing death for the first time with the loss of my mother. It was unexpected. It was tragic. It was my first taste of grief. From the second I heard that she was gone, I honestly expected that I would never laugh again.

At first I even thought that I would cry forever. Literally. When the first tear fell, I can remember thinking, "This is it.

This is what my life will consist of from now on. I will never do anything else other than cry and sleep."

That idea proved wrong when the tears gradually stopped flowing. I realized that it is physically impossible to cry forever, but until that time, I had no idea. I had always thought that your tears must flow in direct proportion to the severity of your grief. If something happened that you would grieve forever, then you would likely cry forever too.

But eternal tears do not exist. That was my first lesson.

I adjusted my thinking accordingly and figured that if I couldn't physically cry forever, then I would just internally cry forever. I would never experience any emotion other than sadness, and I would never think any thought other than about my loss.

Imagine my surprise when that theory proved false as well. I had made it through about two days of pure, uninterrupted grief, which climaxed at the funeral service that somehow managed to squeeze out even more tears from my deceivingly dry eyes. Surrounded by a house full of mourners and well wishers, I was back on the road to my new life of emotional numbness.

That's when I heard the familiar sound. *Laughter.* It sounded so out of place at first. So inappropriate. So distant.

Then it hit me. *I* was the one laughing.

I panicked. Somehow, I had seen or heard something funny, and in a moment of sheer weakness, I allowed a giggle to sneak out. "What would my mother think?" I wondered. Here I was supposed to be mourning her death, and suddenly I was laughing instead.

I quickly looked around to see if anyone had noticed my disrespectful display, but that's when I saw that I was not the only one. Others were laughing as well. I learned that grief was not at all what I expected. Apparently, life continues, you move on, and eventually you laugh again.

Holding Out for a Hero

In the last chapter, we looked at JD's grief. When tragedy struck, she didn't slap on a fake smile and hide behind platitudes of "It'll be okay," and "God has a plan." Instead, she ran to the mountains and cried her heart out to God. If her actions comforted you when we studied her grief, they will absolutely inspire you when we study her guarantee.

In one single move, she carried out the most honorable, most courageous, and most difficult action of her young life.

She returned to her father.

Do you sense the weight of those words? *She went back!* She moved on. She dried her tears, washed her face, and confronted her grief head-on by honoring her guarantee to return to her father.

I hope you don't think that this was an easy decision for her to make.

The life that awaited her at the bottom of the mountain was a *hard* life. It was one of tragedy, disappointment, and undesirable circumstances. Do you think she *wanted* to rush back home to a life like that? Of course not! But here's where JD once again proves to be exceptional—she did it anyway.

Again I have to wonder about what was going through our heroine's mind when the end of her two-month escape drew near. Did she think about hiding? Did she consider running away? Did she ever entertain the false hope that maybe her father would refuse to go through with it?

If it were I, I would have naively hoped for the storybook rescue to save me from my fate. After all, a hero on horseback always complements a damsel in distress. With the precarious position of our heroine, the scene was set quite perfectly for such climactic heroics.

JD had been away for two months. The news of the triumph over the Ammonites had no doubt reached every household. The Israelites were probably still celebrating the victory, but under the constant noise of excitement and energy, a soft murmur quickly spread throughout the land. Much like the soft whisper of a rumor, the murmuring started out softly but grew louder over time. Could it be true? Could Jephthah, the very hero whose actions they were celebrating, actually have promised his daughter as a sacrifice?

The townspeople wouldn't believe it at first. There was no way such an honorable man could do something so despicable. He was too respectable, and she had too much potential. But if it wasn't true, then where was JD?

But then (and this is where my imagination takes off a bit), the news of JD's destiny reached *him*—the handsome and wealthy landowner with sun-kissed skin, perfect manners, and a winning smile. Every eligible female had her eyes on him, but he had eyes only for JD.

He had admired her from afar for longer than he'd been willing to admit but had finally determined in his heart that she was the woman for him. He was just about to approach her father when the war began. Since then, he had been biding his time until the war was over, her father returned, and he could properly ask for her hand in marriage.

If the rumors he heard in town were true, then he had to do

something about it. In an instant, he mounted his black—no wait—make that his white horse and set off to find Jephthah and demand some answers.

After a heated argument, the truth was confirmed, and our hero knew what he had to do. He took off for the mountain, where he knew JD usually went when she was upset, and searched for her until the sun started dropping. At last he caught a glimpse of her off in the distance, her friends surrounding her like the wall of an impenetrable city.

"JD!" he cried, as their eyes locked and his trusty steed began galloping towards her. "Grab my hand!" he shouted when he was near, and in one smooth motion, he whisked her off the ground and landed her safely beside him. Together, they rode off into the sunset burying her so-called destiny in the dust as her tambourine created the perfect accompaniment to the percussion of his horse's gallops . . .

If only it had ended that way.

Holding Out for a Ram

Alas, there would be no knight in shining armor for JD, but then she knew that already. Whether she daydreamed or not during her time in the mountains, it didn't delay the two-month deadline. When the sixty days were up, her time of grief ended, and her guarantee began.

Do you think she was the one to make the call? "Okay girls. It's been two months. It's time to go home."

Or do you suppose they had to tell her? "JD, it's over now. We have to get back or your father will come looking for you."

From what we know about JD, I don't think the girls had to

remind her of anything. She led those girls to the mountains, and I'm pretty sure she led them back home as well.

"Are you sure you're ready, JD?" the girls asked.

"I'm sure I'll never be *ready*," she replied, "but I'm also sure I need to go anyway."

JD knew that her obedience would not lead to a different outcome. Her fate was still sealed, and not even by honoring her guarantee would she be able to change that. "And he did to her as he had vowed" (v. 39). She went back home, and her father fulfilled his vow.

End of story.

If you're like me, you might begin to feel a little uncomfortable at this point-of-no-return in the story. If you weren't holding out for a hero, some of you were probably at least holding out for a ram, like the one God provided for Abraham when he promised to sacrifice his son, Isaac.

Why didn't God provide a ram in this case?

JD had already proven herself. She respected her father. She honored him. She was willing to obey him no matter the cost. Wasn't that enough? What else was there to prove? Since she had reached contentment in her circumstances, wasn't God supposed to reward her by saving her from them?

Some of you have used the same logic about your own life. Perhaps you went through a rough time when you were a little upset with God that you weren't married yet. You read the Bible. You read other books for singles. And then you finally reached that point of contentment. God had not yet provided a husband for you, and for the first time ever you could honestly say that you were okay with that.

But now, a few Christmases later, you're *still* single.

Where is the reward in that?

Unfortunately, this feeling is the result of a lie that you've probably heard at least once in your single life. I know I've heard it a time or two. "Once you're satisfied with being single, *that's* when you'll finally meet someone."

> God's ways cannot be summed up in a nice, neat little formula. His plans are far too creative to be that predictable.

What variation of the lie have you been told?

Somehow, even in Christian circles, this belief that our God is formulaic is gaining popularity. If we follow whichever predetermined special formula is the trend of the moment, then we'll get whatever we're looking for. Wealth. Success. Marriage. Children.

But do you really think our God is small enough to fit inside a formula like that? "'For my thoughts are not your thoughts, neither are your ways my ways,' declares the LORD. 'As the heavens are higher than the earth, so are my ways higher than your ways and my thoughts than your thoughts'" (Isaiah 55:8–9).

God's ways cannot be summed up in a nice, neat little formula. His plans are far too creative to be that predictable. In the end, He is God and we are not. He does not have to answer to us. He never has, and He never will. Whatever the situation, His prerogative trumps our own.

If your guarantee to obey God is conditional upon His "coming through for you" on your terms, I would suggest you brace yourself for a reality check. God works on *His* terms, not yours. Sometimes He provides a ram; sometimes He does not.

Getting Up and Moving On

In JD's case, her grief did not end with the cinematic fanfare that a rescue would have provided. Instead, her grief ended with action. *Her* action. Her father did not have to come and find her to bring her home. Her friends did not have to drag her by the hand back down the mountain. Instead, she grieved, then she got up.

I am reminded of Hannah's grief in the first chapter of 1 Samuel. Hannah grieved because she could not have any children, and children were the desire of her heart, much like marriage was the desire of JD's heart. But year after year, she remained barren.

"In bitterness of soul Hannah wept much and prayed to the LORD" (v. 10). She grieved with so much emotion that the priest in the temple thought that she was drunk! When she quickly explained, "I have not been drinking wine or beer; I was pouring out my soul to the LORD" (v. 15), the priest understood and blessed her. "Then she went her way and ate something" (v. 18).

Hannah ended her grief with a very simple action: She ate something. Just like JD, she grieved, then she got up. In her case, eating was the first step in moving beyond her grief.

Over time, Hannah's prayers were answered, and the Lord blessed her with a little boy. She named him Samuel, and God used him in mighty ways. He was dedicated as the Lord's servant from birth, but even he learned a lesson in moving beyond grief.

The Lord used Samuel as His prophet, and Samuel anointed Saul as the very first king over Israel. Samuel had high hopes that Saul would eventually prove worthy of the elite position in which he had been placed, but Saul continued to disappoint him. It grieved Samuel that Saul was not the king he should be, and eventually the Lord rejected Saul as king and ended his reign.

"Until the day Samuel died, he did not go to see Saul again, though Samuel mourned for him" (1 Samuel 15:35). Saul's actions crushed Samuel, and he wept over the fallen king by pouring his heart out to God. God completely understood Samuel's grief, and the Bible even says that God grieved as well. But the time came when the grief had to end.

"The LORD said to Samuel, 'How long will you mourn for Saul, since I have rejected him as king over Israel? Fill your horn with oil and be on your way'" (1 Samuel 16:1). Samuel couldn't mourn forever; there was still work that God needed him to do. In a sense, God had to tell him, "Okay, you've grieved. Now get up! Move beyond your grief!"

It is not important *how* you move beyond the grief, but *that* you move beyond it. Consider Jesus once again and His prayer in the Garden of Gethsemane. He got down on His knees and poured His heart out to God three times that His circumstances would change. He grieved so hard that His sweat was like blood dripping from His forehead.

JD got up and returned to her father. Hannah got up and ate something. Samuel got up and filled his horn with oil.

Jesus got up and went to the cross.

Finding Purpose in Your Tears

Your grief over being single is no different from any other trying situation. God welcomes your tears, but He doesn't want you to cry forever. Remember, grief that sits for too long usually begins fermenting and turns to whine anyway, so whether you feel ready or not, there comes a time when you've got to get up. God has a plan for you, but if you're constantly looking at your life through your tears, His plan is going to look awfully blurry.

In the last chapter, we talked about how grief can turn to joy when we shift our focus away from ourselves and onto God. The same can be said for turning grief into action. A great way to start is by focusing on God.

"When times are good, be happy; but when times are bad, consider: God has made the one as well as the other" (Ecclesiastes 7:14). The first thing to remember is that God made today. It doesn't matter if you're having a good day or a bad day; He still made today. In fact, He made yesterday, and if tomorrow comes, it will be because He made that too.

And because He made today, nothing about the events of today can surprise Him. You could be having the most terrible, the most rotten, the most disappointing Tuesday you've ever seen, and it will not phase Him one bit. He *made* Tuesday. He's prepared for whatever Tuesday has to offer. Not only do the details not shake Him, but He already has a plan to use Tuesday's terrible moments for another day's wonderful moments. God is resourceful like that.

> God has a plan for you, but if you're constantly looking at your life through your tears, His plan is going to look awfully blurry.

You've probably had Romans 8:28 quoted to you before, as it is often another one of the stereotypical verses of encouragement for singles. I debated even mentioning it in this chapter because I think that sometimes people quote it as more of a cliché than as a promise from God. Nevertheless, its truth is so powerful that I couldn't ignore it, and you shouldn't ignore it either. "And we know that in all things God works for the good of those who love him, who have been called according to his purpose."

God never says that all things are good. He never says that all days are good days. He simply promises that He can use every day for something good.

Being single, you may not cook often, but I'm sure you have at least made a batch of cookies before. Have you ever considered the ingredients that go into cookies? Raw eggs, flour, melted butter, baking soda. Independently, any of those ingredients would taste disgusting. But somehow, when the gross ingredients mix with some good ones, like sugar and vanilla and chocolate chips, a miraculous transformation occurs. No longer do you have a row of ingredients that taste horrible and another row that taste great. Instead you have a final product that is delicious—chocolate chip cookies!

God never claims that you won't get a few raw eggs. He just promises that if you'll let Him, He'll use those disgusting raw eggs to make you yummy, mouth-watering cookies.

Someone who knew a thing or two about raw eggs in Old Testament times was Joseph. After his glory days when he made famous the coat of many colors, he endured more than his share of bad days. He was sold into slavery by his brothers, falsely accused by Potiphar's wife, and thrown into jail as an innocent man. But God used each of those unfortunate events and stirred them all into Joseph's life to yield something wonderful. Joseph became second-in-command over all of Egypt and successfully led the nation through seven years of famine. When Joseph's brothers tried to apologize for their part in his days of misfortune, he wouldn't even let them finish. "You intended to harm me, but God intended it for good to accomplish what is now being done, the saving of many lives" (Genesis 50:20).

Joseph basically told his brothers not to worry about the grief they had caused him. He had turned it all into action.

March Forth

I learned a wonderful life lesson from my friends, Ross and Mandy. A few years ago, Mandy was pregnant with their second child, Oliver Thomas. Everything was going well until late in the pregnancy when the doctor discovered that little Ollie was not as healthy as they hoped. Three weeks later Mandy went in for her checkup, and her doctor checked her into the hospital for immediate delivery via c-section. Little Ollie was born at 7:31 p.m. on Tuesday, March 4, and he lived for twenty-five minutes.

A few weeks later, I received an e-mail from Ross reflecting on the short life of his little boy. He and Mandy were still grieving their terrible loss, but they had found peace in the midst of their sorrow.

If nothing else, you can find purpose in your tears simply by knowing that you will be able to be a blessing to someone else who goes through a situation similar to yours.

March 4th, they explained, was not just the date of their son's birth and death. It was also a command. March *forth*. Press onward. Move beyond your grief.

Ross and Mandy knew that God was not at all surprised at the events of that random, terrible day. God made March 4, remember? So they turned right back around and gave God that day, along with their grief, and He immediately used their story to bless others.

If nothing else, you can find purpose in your tears simply by knowing that you will be able to be a blessing to someone else who goes through a situation similar to yours. "Praise be to the God and Father of our Lord Jesus Christ, the Father of compassion and the God of all comfort, who comforts us in all our troubles, so that we can comfort those in any trouble with the comfort we ourselves have received from God" (2 Corinthians 1:3–4).

God gave me comfort over my grief of being single. He wrapped His arms around me, let me cry on His shoulder, and at the perfect time, pointed me back to the obscure story of Jephthah's daughter. He used this unnamed girl, who lived in another land and another age, to comfort a twenty-first-century wife wannabe. In a sense, I ended up writing this book because of what I learned from JD's guarantee to return home to her father. She followed her time of mourning with action; God called me to do the same when He called me to write this book for you.

I received comfort from her story, and I chose to pass that comfort on to you. To whom will you pass on your comfort? How will you turn your grief into action?

Your Guarantee

1. Let your imagination run wild. If you could rewrite the ending to JD's story, how might it turn out?

2. Read about Abraham's promise to sacrifice Isaac in Genesis 22:1–14. Now reread the story of Jephthah's daughter in Judges 11:30–40. Why do you think God provides a ram in one instance and not in the other?

3. Now focus specifically on the first part of each story in Genesis 22:1 and Judges 11:30–31. Who was testing whom in Abraham's story? Who was testing whom in Jephthah's story? Might that have anything to do with why God provided a ram for Abraham and not for Jephthah? What does Deuteronomy 6:16 say about testing God?

4. Read Philippians 4:12, where Paul says that he has learned the secret of being content. What do you think the secret of contentment is? What does the following verse, verse 13, teach about contentment?

5. Read John 5:1–9. What reason did the man in the story have to grieve? What command did Jesus give him? If the man had not obeyed Jesus, do you think his grief would still have ended?

6. According to Romans 8:28, all things are not good, but all things can work together for good. Describe a time in your

life when God brought something good from something unpleasant.

7. Look at 2 Corinthians 1:3–4 again. Have you ever had a situation in which God comforted you through His Word, a song, or a special word from a friend? Were you able to pass that comfort on to someone else? How? If not, how might you be able to pass on that comfort now?

8. *Memorize* Isaiah 55:8–9: "'For my thoughts are not your thoughts, neither are your ways my ways,' declares the LORD. 'As the heavens are higher than the earth, so are my ways higher than your ways and my thoughts than your thoughts.'"

Chapter 11

Her Guiltlessness

And she was a virgin (Judges 11:39).

Problems of Innocence

My decision to major in English in college was not a difficult one. With my love of all things literary, I could hardly wait for my first college English courses to begin. I knew they would be difficult, but I also knew that I was enough of a nerd not to mind.

I took my first literature course the spring semester of my freshman year. With Comp I and Comp II already behind me, I felt prepared and eager for a semester of analyzing and explicating the works of some of the great English writers.

But nothing prepared me for what I discovered the first week.

Most of the students in the class had also been in my composition classes, and the same professor taught both, so by the second class, we were already up to our pocket protectors in the poetry of T. S. Eliot. "What does this stanza symbolize?" the professor asked, referring to a stanza from *The Love Song of J. Alfred Prufrock*. I read it again to myself, certain that all lines were pointing towards an animal of some sort. A cat perhaps? Maybe a dog?

I was just about to answer when a know-it-all in the front of the room raised her hand. "I think this stanza is talking about sex," she said.

I was embarrassed for the girl, who usually had such keen observations, but couldn't help smirking a little that she was so off course. I was about to enlighten her with my wisdom when the professor exclaimed, "That's exactly right! Line by line, this stanza perfectly symbolizes the act of sex, from beginning to end."

A loud and very high-pitched, "What?" escaped my mouth as I grabbed my book and held it directly under my nose to re-read it. Sex? I thought the poem was about a cat!

The professor started laughing at my outburst and shook his head. "Emily," he said, "you are way too innocent."

Over the next few years, I often went back to that professor's comment about my innocence, and there were many times when I was tempted to agree with him. I quickly caught on that a lot, if not most, of the literature that we studied had sexual undertones. The question I started asking myself was no longer, "What does this symbolize?" but rather, "How does this symbolize sex?"

The theme spread into my other classes as well. In biology, we studied sex from a physical standpoint. In philosophy, we debated the ethical implications of sex. In psychology, we studied the physiological stages of sex.

I couldn't help but wonder if my classes would be easier if I were more "experienced." I know that sounds extreme, but what harm could it do? The professors taught sex like we knew what they were talking about, and it seemed to come up *all the time.* Semester after semester, my professor's voice kept ringing in my ears.

Maybe I *was* too innocent.

The Urgency for Intimacy

There were times when I was teased so mercilessly for my inexperience that I could think of nothing worse than to go down in history like JD had: "And she was a virgin" (Judges 11:39). When you read these words the first time, you're not quite sure if they're a compliment or an insult. Are they complimenting the fact that JD remained pure and guiltless with her body, or are they highlighting, once again, the reality that JD would never be married and never have children?

When it comes to sex, Satan has a whole arsenal of weapons that he can use against us. Getting us to believe that purity is an insult is just one of his weapons.

I expected that after I was out of college and not surrounded by classes and professors that related everything to sex, I would not be tempted to consider innocence as a weakness. But that wasn't the case. I realized I couldn't even watch prime-time television without getting bombarded by a slew of sexual jokes and innuendoes.

And most of them, I didn't understand.

Satan loves to build up sex as the ultimate mystery. He deceives us into thinking that we're outsiders until we've solved the mystery, and the quicker we discover the secrets of sex, the quicker we'll be included in the "inside jokes" of the world.

Tick . . .

Tock . . .

Aside from the mystery factor, another weapon Satan uses against us is the biological factor. For those who want to be moms someday, there is the fear that the longer you wait to try to have a baby, the more likely you are to incur fertility problems. When you start counting backwards from menopause, it's scary to realize just how few "good" years you have left.

Tick . . .

Tock . . .

For others, there is the touch factor that Satan uses to create urgency. Whether it's the sexual desire to be aroused or the emotional desire to be held, the need for touch seems almost as strong as the need for water at times. He deceives us into thinking that physical desires need to be met with the same urgency as physical needs, like the need for food and water, and that they need to be met *now*.

Tick . . .

Tock . . .

Do you think that Jephthah's daughter felt the urgency too? When her father returned home and the details of his vow were revealed, JD had only two months until her life, as she knew it, was over. Time was *not* on her side. Whether you're twenty-four or forty-four, you can probably empathize with her feeling of urgency as you face your own battles with the mystery factor, the biological factor, and the touch factor.

After college I attended a church that boasts one of the largest singles ministries in Texas. I didn't join with the ulterior motive of "husband hunting," but I figured it couldn't hurt to be around plenty of "possibilities" as I worshiped God. One of the first sermons I remember hearing at the church was a sermon on marriage. The pastor talked about the statistics of marriage and how, over the years, people are getting married later and later in life. "In our church, the average age of marriage is about four to five years higher than the national average," he told the congregation.

> When God commands purity, He gives us the very strength we need to remain pure.

Higher?

So I had joined a church with thousands of singles that were waiting *longer* to get married? What was wrong with these people? Didn't they know that time was running out? Weren't their hormones raging? Couldn't they hear their biological clocks ticking?

What about JD, for that matter? Didn't she contemplate giving in to a moment of weakness before she committed her life to fulfill her father's vow? Couldn't she hear her clock ticking too?

Or is it possible that her tambourine was loud enough to drown out such background noise?

The Passion for Purity

Jephthah's daughter was cemented into history with the words that proclaimed her purity: "And she was a virgin," and again I ask, is this statement a compliment or an insult?

When God commands purity, He gives us the very strength we need to remain pure. "The God of Israel gives power and

strength to his people" (Psalm 68:35). So without a doubt, these
words are a compliment.

Guiltlessness has to begin in your mind.

JD was a girl very similar to you and to me. She was not immune to passion. She wanted to get married, and she wanted to have sex. Many versions of the Bible even say that she *bewailed* her virginity.

But in the end, she let God—not her hormones, not a boy-friend, and not a sense of urgency—determine when and if she would experience physical intimacy. She did not sacrifice her purity for her passion, and she remained guiltless until the end.

Guiltlessness is not merely an absence of fornication; rather it is the presence of purity. It is submitting your urges and desires to God's authority and striving to maintain a state of innocence. For this reason, guiltlessness cannot begin in the bedroom or on the couch or in the back of a car. Guiltlessness has to begin in your mind.

Second Corinthians 10:5 says that we should, "take captive every thought to make it obedient to Christ." What would God say about your thought life? Does it strive for purity? Does it seek to shield itself from the influences of the world and maintain a state of innocence? What about your thoughts of, "How far is too far?" Do you spend as much time wondering about your date's spiritual maturity as you do about how much physical activity is allowed?

What about your thought of, "I'll get on the pill *just in case*." In case what? Would God be pleased that you're entertaining even the possibility of sex when He clearly tells us to "flee from sexual immorality" (1 Corinthians 6:18)?

Fleeing immorality means more than just abstaining from the

act of intercourse. It means that you don't even *think* about it. It means that if your mind entertains even a hint of anything impure, you consciously and quickly turn those thoughts around.

"After desire has conceived, it gives birth to sin; and sin, when it is full-grown, gives birth to death" (James 1:15). Sin is a process, not an isolated event. It begins with a thought, it strengthens with curiosity, and it culminates with action. For that reason God urges us to flee at the *first sign* of sin.

Gagged and Dragged

It was almost midnight on a Friday night when God illustrated this command for me.

I was returning home from a church social with my friend, Jennifer, when we were stopped at a traffic light just a block away from home. We were both fighting sleep and didn't even notice the black BMW in front of us until the trunk slowly opened, and a boy, clad only in duct tape and blue boxer shorts, climbed out of it.

His hands were bound, his mouth was taped shut, and his eyes were wide with fear. He took a split second to survey his surroundings and then dashed across oncoming traffic racing towards a nearby neighborhood. Seconds later, two boys from inside the BMW flung open their doors and chased after him, one waving a baseball bat high over his head as he ran.

My need for sleep was forgotten; my heart was pounding; and I grabbed my cell phone to dial 9-1-1. I followed the car just long enough to report the license plate, then turned around to look for the boy.

We drove around the neighborhood looking for any sign of

the boy or the BMW but never saw either. After making the block a few times, we were stopped at the same traffic light as before when we finally saw the car again. Across the street in a restaurant parking lot, two police cars turned on their lights and cornered the black BMW. From around the corner, three more police cars appeared on the scene, surrounding the BMW and making it impossible for the boys to escape. The policemen got out, guns drawn, and approached the car slowly.

Meanwhile, Jennifer and I watched from a distance and shouted with joy as the scene unfolded. "Look! They're pulling the boys out of the car," I screamed as the police officers lined the boys along the side of the BMW and slammed their hands on the hood.

"They caught them! They caught them!" yelled Jennifer. Then the evening climaxed as a policeman opened the trunk of the car, revealing the same half-naked, scared little boy inside. They helped him out of the trunk as Jennifer and I bounced up and down in victory, celebrating that the boy was finally safe and that we had been instrumental in his release.

That night God showed me what it looked like to flee from sin. When Christians face temptation, we should be like the little boy who was locked in the trunk.

That boy had to be *forced* into the trunk. He had to be bound, gagged, and dragged into captivity before the hood of the trunk slammed down on top of him. And once inside, he didn't give up and accept defeat. Instead, as soon as the first opportunity to escape presented itself, he took off running as far and as quickly as he could away from his captors.

The Bible says, "each one is tempted when, by his own evil desire, he is dragged away and enticed" (James 1:14). James thought awfully highly of us when he said that we had to be "dragged away and enticed" into sin. Often that's not the case at all.

How many times do we make it easy for Satan to lure us into his trunk of sin, especially into the trunk of sexual sin? He doesn't always have to bind us. He doesn't have to force us or drag us into temptation. Often all he does is *suggest* we get in the trunk, and we hop on in voluntarily and close the hood for him.

We should approach the possibility of falling into temptation with the same amount of drive and determination as we would if someone were trying to lock us into the trunk of a car. We should fight it! We should run from it! And at the very first chance, we should escape it!

"No temptation has seized you except what is common to man. And God is faithful; he will not let you be tempted beyond what you can bear. But when you are tempted, he will also provide a way out so that you can stand up under it" (1 Corinthians 10:13).

Maybe you're locked in a trunk of impurity right now, and you've given up any hope of a way out. Maybe you climbed in voluntarily at the devil's mere suggestion, or maybe you were dragged away and enticed. Either way, know that God promises that there is *always* a way out. There is a safety latch

> It is not enough to clear your mind of impure thoughts. You must also fill it with pure thoughts.

on the inside of that trunk, and you can escape. You don't have to remain trapped in sin any longer.

Running Towards Purity

Nevertheless, as important as it is to consider what you're running away from, it is not as important as what you're running *towards*. It is not enough to clear your mind of impure thoughts. You must also fill it with pure thoughts.

"Finally, brothers, whatever is true, whatever is noble, whatever is right, whatever is pure, whatever is lovely, whatever is admirable—if anything is excellent or praiseworthy—think about such things" (Philippians 4:8).

You should ponder questions of righteousness. You should seek out truth. You should consistently praise God in your heart.

If your goal for purity is merely to wait until you're married to have sex, then you're not setting your standards high enough. Your standard should be holiness! "For God did not call us to be impure, but to live a holy life" (1 Thessalonians 4:7).

Thankfully, it is never too late to run towards purity. Because purity includes so much more than just virginity, it's probably safe to assume that we all need help in this area. Purity before (and during) marriage is God's best plan for us, but since we have fallen short of that ultimate goal, in thought or in action, God promises forgiveness. In Isaiah 43:25, God says, "I, even I, am he who blots out your transgressions, for my own sake, and remembers your sins no more."

It doesn't matter if you messed up once or once a weekend, if you've had one sexual partner or several. Our God is a God of forgiveness, and His grace is the springboard for second chances (and third chances and fourth).

Maybe you've never *done* anything impure, but you're guilty of impure thoughts. God's forgiveness reaches to you as well.

Remember what we learned about grace in chapter 5. Because of God's grace, not only are our sins forgiven, we also receive Christ's righteousness. Once you've asked God to forgive you for being impure, He no longer sees those sins when He looks at you. Instead, He looks at you and sees the purity of Christ.

In order to run towards purity, run towards Christ. "For it is written: 'Be holy, because I am holy'" (1 Peter 1:16).

Pointing Each Other Towards Purity

We all have many improvements to make in our quest for guiltlessness and purity. Will we help each other, or will we make it harder for each other?

Hebrews 10:24 says, "And let us consider how we may spur one another on toward love and good deeds." As you determine in your heart to run towards purity, are you also considering how you can encourage others in the same endeavor?

I will never forget Michelle, a woman who encouraged me in my quest for purity. She was the wife of my youth minister in high school, and she shared her testimony with the entire youth ministry a few months after their wedding.

I could tell that she was nervous as she began talking about her engagement to her husband. They both believed that God designed sex as something to be shared between a man and his wife, she explained. And though it wasn't always easy, they both remained virgins until their wedding night.

In her soft voice, she shared what a blessing their obedience had meant to their marriage. She spoke about their purity with such conviction, and with tears in her eyes, she pleaded with us to do the same.

I had heard emotional pleas about purity before, but they usually came from the testimony of one who had repented from her impurity rather than from one who had been blessed because of her purity.

Because of her passion for purity, Michelle made an impact in my own guiltlessness.

Some say that passion and purity cannot coexist. Michelle's testimony proved otherwise for me.

JD's story proves otherwise as well.

In this sexually saturated world, are you running towards purity, guiltlessness, and holiness? Are you encouraging others to run with you?

Your Guiltlessness

1. Have you ever experienced a situation in which you thought you were too innocent? Have you ever felt like you were not innocent enough?

2. Can you think of a situation in your life or in that of a friend's when the word *virgin* (or something similar) was used as an insult? As a compliment?

3. What do 2 Corinthians 5:17 and Romans 8:1–2 say about second chances?

4. According to 1 Corinthians 6:18–20, how is sexual sin different from other sins? Verse 20 says that you were bought with a price. Consider *who* paid the price and *how* the price was paid. How does this change or confirm your thoughts about sex?

5. Romans 7:15–20 is a great passage that talks about our desire to be guiltless versus our tendencies to keep sinning. Read the passage several times, then put it in your own words.

6. Read 1 Corinthians 10:12–13. What are two promises that God gives us as we face temptation?

7. Hebrews 10:24 says that we are to "spur one another on toward love and good deeds." What are some practical ways that you can do this regarding the subject of sex?

8. *Memorize* 1 Peter 1:15–16: "But just as he who called you is holy, so be holy in all you do; for it is written: 'Be holy, because I am holy.'"

Chapter 12

Her Guidance

From this comes the Israelite custom that each year the young women of Israel go out for four days to commemorate the daughter of Jephthah the Gileadite (Judges 11:39–40).

Reluctant Leadership

At the time, it sounded like a good idea: spending the summer as a counselor at a Christian camp in east Texas. The thought of being able to mentor young girls while working on my tan sounded like a great opportunity. I signed up in early March and couldn't wait for June to begin.

Unfortunately, the day before I left for camp, my boyfriend and I unexpectedly broke up. Suddenly I went from feeling prepared and excited about my new service venture to feeling depressed, lonely, and apathetic. During the first two weeks of camp, when the counselors go through training before the first set of campers arrives, I thought many times about calling it quits and going home. Not only did I cry every day because of the breakup, I also took a fall and bruised my ribs, spent a couple of days in the infirmary, and, as a result, failed my lifeguard certification test.

The day before the campers arrived, my body was still extremely sore, my spirit was dejected, and my emotional state was iffy, to say the least. With all that had gone on, I was in no shape to guide and influence young minds.

"God, why did You bring me here when You knew how unprepared I would be?" I asked as I stomped through the thick woods on my way to my new home in the Navajo cabin. "I should be spending my post-breakup months at home, where my parents could comfort me and my sister could watch sappy movies with me while I nursed my broken heart. I should not be stuck out in the woods, with no friends and no link to the outside world, thinking about how to keep a cabin full of ten-year-old girls entertained for a week at a time."

Comfort did not come right away, and neither did a way out. So I braced myself for the first week of girls and determined to suffer through the rest of the summer.

Miraculously, I connected with at least one of my young campers week after week. First there was little Emily, with her long straggly hair and thick glasses. She latched on to me from the beginning, simply because we shared the same name, and for that reason alone I was able to talk to her about Jesus. Next came soft-spoken Melissa, who would hardly say two words to any of the counselors at first. But when it came to water sports, she was a scaredy cat just like me, so we were able to spend several afternoons talking by the pool as we watched everyone else play in the water.

It wasn't until week three or so, when I caught the bubbly

blonde Ashlee crying in the bathroom because her "camp boy-friend," Robbie, had just dumped her, that I finally realized why God had brought me to camp Sky Ranch. It wasn't so I could impress the masses of preteen girls with my quick wit or hip personality. It was so that God could use me to reach the one lost sheep in every herd of campers.

Every Sunday brought a new group of girls, and I didn't have anything to offer them of myself because I was on empty. But I could offer them Jesus. And looking back, I realize that that must have been God's plan all along. He didn't want to use me because of who I was. He wanted to use me in spite of who I was.

Her Guidance

It's easy to shy away from leadership when you're going through the valley. Many times it feels like you're not able to give help or encouragement because you need it so much yourself. "How can I serve others when everything in my own life seems so uncertain? How can I guide them to the truth when I still need someone to follow myself?"

Learning to serve in spite of our circumstances and in spite of who we are can sometimes be the most difficult lesson for us to learn. So often we'd rather wait until we're "ready." Until we know enough, until we've experienced enough, until the ups and downs of our lives have finally leveled out.

Really, we would prefer to wait until it's convenient.

I wonder if it was "convenient" for JD to set such a high exam-ple for the young women of Israel when she was going through the valley. Apparently she made quite an impression on the girls around her—so much of an impression that they remembered her year after year and set aside a long weekend to honor her. "From this comes the Israelite custom that each year the young women of Israel go out for four days to commemorate the daughter of Jephthah the Gileadite" (Judges 11:39–40).

In today's world, when someone exhibits a heroic act of leadership, she might get a parade in her honor or a high school named after her or maybe even her birthday turned into a local holiday. When JD returned to her father to fulfill his vow and to face her destiny, she received recognition for her service as well. If she lived in today's times, someone probably would have displayed her tambourine in a museum for all to see. Her actions set the standard and raised the bar for future generations to come as she guided them with her obedience.

The ending of JD's story is the beginning of her legacy. She led the welcome-home ceremony, and then she led the girls to the mountains with her tears. They followed her back home after meeting with God, and we follow her example today after reading her story.

How did she become so influential that the girls in her town commemorated her each year? How did she leave such a mark that we're reading about her thousands of years later and still finding inspiration? And, more importantly, how can we lead lives that provide lasting guidance for others like she did?

Before You Serve

When it comes to making a mark on the lives of others by serving God, there is only one "rule" to start with, and we can find it by studying the greatest servant of all, Jesus. In each of the four Gospels, each writer gives his own account of how Jesus began His earthly ministry. It was a ministry that involved teaching, calling disciples, and performing many miracles. However, before He did any of these things, the Bible is clear on one important fact: Jesus was baptized.

"Then Jesus came from Galilee to the Jordan to be baptized by John. But John tried to deter him, saying, 'I need to be baptized by you, and do you come to me?' Jesus replied, 'Let it be so now; it is proper for us to do this to fulfill all righteousness.' Then John consented" (Matthew 3:13–15).

> God does not want anything from you—your service, your money, your talents, or anything else —until He has *you* first.

Baptism is an outward reflection of an inward transformation. The act itself does not save us; it simply shows everyone around us what has already taken place in our hearts. It symbolizes our dying to our old ways of life and rising again to walk with Christ. Jesus did not need to die to His old life because He was perfect and sinless in every way. But He still went through the act of baptism as an example to all of us.

The order of His actions shows us exactly how God wants us to serve Him as well. If you read in any of the four Gospels, you will see that Jesus did not perform any recorded miracles, preach any sermons, or minister in any other way until *after* He was baptized and received the Holy Spirit. God does not want anything from you—your service, your money, your talents, or anything else—until He has *you* first.

God wants you to serve Him. He wants you to minister to others in whatever unique ways in which He has equipped you. But, more than anything else, He wants your heart first.

If God doesn't have your heart, focus all of your energy and attention on giving it to Him before you begin ministering to others.

Qualifications of Service

Once God has your heart, there are only three words you need to know to be qualified for leadership: "Here I am."

You may feel a little disappointed that there's not more. Maybe you've always thought that you shouldn't serve until you had a certain number of Bible verses memorized. Or perhaps someone has told you that you need to know exactly what spiritual gifts you have before you begin ministering to others.

Maybe you haven't been a Christian long enough. Maybe you've been a Christian so long that it's too late for you to begin serving now. Maybe you've never read the whole Bible through. Maybe you don't understand the Trinity.

Surely there are more qualifications than just, "Here I am."

If you think that you have to be "qualified" for God to use you, then you don't understand how God works. People do not do great and mighty things for God; God does great and mighty things through people. "For we are God's workmanship, created in Christ Jesus to do good works, which God prepared in advance for us to do" (Ephesians 2:10). God has made every preparation necessary to further His kingdom. He is the giver of talents, the giver of strength, the giver of circumstances. He doesn't need you to be *able*; He needs you to be *available*.

If you notice in Scripture, God rarely chose the most qualified person for assignments of leadership. Instead, He chose a shepherd boy to be king, He chose fishermen to be disciples, and He chose a virgin to be the mother of Christ. God looked past their abilities and saw their availability.

> He wants to use you now, and all He's waiting for is to hear you say, "Here I am."

Next time you hear the stories of Abraham, Jacob, Moses, or Samuel, try to look past their traditional place of renown in Scripture and consider instead how their stories began:

- *Abraham:* "Some time later God tested Abraham. He said to him, 'Abraham!' 'Here I am,' he replied" (Genesis 22:1).
- *Jacob:* "The angel of God said to me in the dream, 'Jacob.' I answered, 'Here I am'" (Genesis 31:11).
- *Moses:* "When the LORD saw that he had gone over to look, God called to him from within the bush, 'Moses! Moses!' And Moses said, 'Here I am'" (Exodus 3:4).
- *Samuel:* "Then the LORD called Samuel. Samuel answered, 'Here I am.'" (1 Samuel 3:4)

The bottom line is that God created you, and He wants to use you. He's not waiting for you to get married to use you. He's not waiting for you to have children or secure the perfect job. He wants to use you *now*, and all He's waiting for is to hear you say, "Here I am."

I love the enthusiasm I see in the words of Isaiah when the Lord called him. "Then I heard the voice of the Lord saying, 'Whom shall I send? And who will go for us?' And I said, 'Here am I. Send me!'" (Isaiah 6:8). I picture Isaiah raising his hand like a schoolboy and yelling, "Ooh, pick me! Pick me!"

Do you hear the voice of the Lord asking, "Whom shall I send?" Then you're qualified to answer, "Here I am."

Supernatural Gifts

In order for God to carry out His supernatural agenda, He must work through His children in supernatural ways. One way He does this is by giving us spiritual gifts through the Holy Spirit.

You've probably heard of spiritual gifts before. Many of you may even know which spiritual gifts you have received. While the list of possible gifts is not set in stone, and a perfect understanding of them is not necessary in order to serve, it can still be helpful to gain a broad understanding of spiritual gifts and how they work.

The first thing to know is that the Holy Spirit distributes spiritual gifts. Because only believers have received the Holy Spirit, it naturally follows that only believers have spiritual gifts. This simple fact alone reiterates that God does not want your service until He has your heart. Once He has your heart, He gives you the Holy Spirit, who in turn gives you one or more spiritual gifts.

Different gifts are mentioned in various places in the New Testament. First Corinthians 12:8–10 mentions the gifts of wisdom, knowledge, faith, and healing, to name a few. Gifts of prophecy, teaching, miracles, helps, and administration are mentioned in 1 Corinthians 12:28. Other gifts appear in Romans 12:6–8; Ephesians 4:11–12; and 1 Peter 4:9–11.

The second thing to note is that spiritual gifts are not the same thing as abilities or talents. You may be a third grade teacher but not have the gift of teaching. You may be a doctor but not have the gift of healing. Or you may be a politician but not have the gift of leadership. Spiritual gifts are given to us for the one purpose of carrying out the work of God. They are supernatural gifts given by a supernatural God for a supernatural agenda.

"There are different kinds of gifts, but the same Spirit. There are different kinds of service, but the same Lord. There are different kinds of working, but the same God works all of them in all men. Now to each one the manifestation of the Spirit is given for the common good" (1 Corinthians 12:4–7).

If you have never explored your own spiritual gifts, I would encourage you to do so soon. It can be a fascinating revelation of how God has wired you for His purposes. While it would be impossible for us to glean a detailed understanding of each and every gift in just a few sections of this chapter, you can search online or go to your local Christian bookstore to research spiritual gifts further.

Gifts, Not Excuses

For those of you who have already determined what your spiritual gifts are, and for the rest of you who plan to determine your gifts soon, one final point must be made. Spiritual gifts are not meant to limit the ways and opportunities for you to serve God. They are meant to give you direction, not ultimatums.

For example, if you discover that you have the gift of teaching, and the next day your coworker's house burns down, there is no reason why you can't offer hospitality to her and let her stay with you for a few nights. You may not have the spiritual gift of hospitality, but you can still serve outside your comfort zone as various opportunities come your way.

Unfortunately, some people discover their spiritual gifts and then use them as excuses not to help in any other venue. They may refuse to give to a special offering because they don't have the gift of giving. They may refuse to forgive someone because they don't have the gift of mercy. And, saddest of all, they may never tell anyone about Jesus because they don't have the gift of evangelism.

Consider this "unabridged" version of the story of the Good Samaritan found in Luke 10:30–35. The words I've added are in italics:

In reply Jesus said: "A man was going down from Jerusalem to Jericho, when he fell into the hands of robbers. They stripped him of his clothes, beat him and went away, leaving him half dead. A priest, *who scored very high in the gifts of evangelism and pastoring*, happened to be going down the same road, and when he saw the man, *he thought to himself, 'Wow. This man sure does need some help. Oh, but wait, that's really not my gift. I'll just leave my business card here, and when he comes to, I'll tell him about the love of Christ and get him involved in a local fellowship.' And* he passed by on the other side. So too, a Levite, *very gifted in teaching and administration*, when he came to the place and saw him, passed by on the other side, *thinking to himself, 'It's too bad I don't have the gift of hospitality. It looks like this guy could really use it right about now.'* But a Samaritan, as he traveled, came where the man was. And *though he did not have the gift of mercy*, when he saw him, he took pity on him. *Despite the fact that he did not have the gift of helps*, he went to him and bandaged his wounds, pouring on oil and wine. Then, *even though hospitality ranked very low on his spiritual gifts list,* he put the man on his own donkey, took him to an inn and took care of him. The next day, *despite the fact that he did not have the gift of giving either,* he took out two silver coins and gave them to the innkeeper. 'Look after him,' he said, 'and when I return, I will reimburse you for any extra expense you may have.'"

Of course the Bible does not reveal the spiritual gifts of any of the people in this story, but you get the point. Spiritual gifts are not excuses. Don't ever miss an opportunity to serve God by saying, "Sorry, that's really not my gift."

But I'm Just Moses

Make no mistake. Serving God can be scary at times. Sometimes the real challenge begins *after* you say, "Here I am!"

Even Moses, the one who led the Israelites out of Egypt, received the Ten Commandments, and wrote the first five books of the Bible, had some hesitations after his very first, "Here I am!"

His story appears in Exodus 3 and 4 when God speaks to him from a burning bush. At first Moses seems eager and willing to serve God. After all, he offers his availability when he answers, "Here I am," in Exodus 3:4. However, the second God tells him how He wants to use him, Moses responds with five excuses why he's not the man for the job.

God's plan is simple. "I am sending you to Pharaoh to bring my people the Israelites out of Egypt" (v. 10). Right away, Moses responds with his first excuse. "Who am I?" he asks in the very next verse.

Self-esteem is the first thing that can get in the way of our service to God. You may think, "Who am I? I'm not a Billy Graham or a Mother Theresa. I'm just a nobody. There's no way God's calling me to do *that!*" Self-esteem can also manifest itself in the form of arrogance. "I'm too valuable to be serving in my tiny little Sunday school class in my tiny little church. God needs me to go national!"

Notice how God responds to Moses. "And God said, 'I will be with you'" (v. 12). He doesn't tell him, "Oh, Moses. You've got so much going for you. You're such a swell guy; I'm sure you can do it." No. He simply says, "I will be with you." In other words, it doesn't matter who you are, because it's not about you anyway. It's about who God is and how He's planning on working through you.

The second phrase of reluctance that escapes Moses' lips is, "Suppose . . ." (v. 13). In this excuse, Moses focuses on his fears, which is something that many of us have done before. For some reason we're scared that God is going to send us out on a battleground with no protection, no ammunition, and no night vision goggles. We're quick to dream up unrealistic worst-case scenarios and forget that the real worst-case scenario is what could happen if we *don't* act.

"God said to Moses, 'I AM WHO I AM'" (v. 14). God calms Moses' fears by reminding him once again who He is. It's not about Moses; it's about "I AM." It's not about you; it's about God.

The third excuse that Moses presents appears in the fourth chapter with two words that should be banned from the lips of all Christians: "What if . . ." (v. 1). Moses is uncertain about the future and therefore reluctant to act in the present.

Sometimes we can be the same way. It's like we expect God to lay out His entire plan of action for us before we're ever even willing to take the first step. We want Him to tell us, "Okay, first we'll begin by turning the water to blood. Then frogs, gnats, flies, livestock, boils, hail, locusts, darkness, and the killing of the firstborn. Finally, we'll reach the climax with the splitting of the Red Sea."

But God doesn't work that way. He responds to Moses by showing him two miracles. First, Moses' rod becomes a snake, and then his hand turns leprous. God never directly answers Moses' concern about the future. He simply reminds him that He is a God of miracles, and He is ready and able to reign victorious over any situation that could possibly come up in the future.

The next excuse Moses presents has to do with his past: "I have never been . . ." (v. 10). In Moses' case, he had never been a dynamic speaker, so he didn't think he could become one now. In our case, we often think with the same logic. If God calls us to do something we've never done before, we automatically assume we can't do it at all.

I love God's response. "Who gave man his mouth? Who makes him deaf or mute? Who gives him sight or makes him blind? Is it not I, the LORD? Now go" (vv. 11–12).

Unfortunately, Moses has one last plea for the Lord, and it is the saddest plea of them all. "Please send someone else," he says in verse 13. Let's face it. Sometimes we, like Moses, just don't want to do what God is calling us to do. We're either tired or burned out or too busy or we just don't care.

Amazingly, God can still use us in spite of who we are. From this conversation at the burning bush, it would seem that Moses was not the best choice to guide the Israelites out of Egypt. He was unqualified, had tons of excuses, and he flat didn't want to do it. But God still used Moses, and he was still successful because God gave him supernatural spiritual gifts that allowed him to carry out the task at hand. By the end of Moses' leadership, he had exhibited signs of administration, wisdom, miracles, teaching, and leadership.

Obedient Leadership

If Moses had known just how much God was going to use him, do you think he would have been encouraged, or do you think he would have come up with even more excuses?

Sometimes I don't know which is scarier: to be used by God or to never be used by God. I've debated that question many times, especially when it comes to this book. I teeter between the possibility that this book never gets published, which is disappointing, frustrating, and relieving all at once, and the possibility that this book actually does get published, which is frightening, humbling, and also a bit relieving. I can't settle on which possibility scares me more.

When it comes to serving God, we can think of a million reasons we shouldn't even attempt such a huge undertaking. But in the end, we need only one reason to go ahead and do it: God tells us to.

Jephthah's daughter did not set out to make a name for herself in the Word of God or to become a scriptural heroine. She simply obeyed God, and He used her obedience to guide others.

Follow her guidance by being obedient to God in service. Then prepare yourself to be amazed at how God uses your obedience to guide, to serve, and to minister to others.

Your Guidance

1. Think of a time when you felt either reluctant or unqualified to serve God. Did you do it anyway? Why or why not? What was the outcome of the situation?

2. Have you ever known someone to leave an impression on your life like JD left on the young women of Israel? Who was that person, and what did he or she do that was so significant to you? What lesson did he or she teach you?

3. Read the following passages and name at least ten different spiritual gifts that appear in the verses: 1 Corinthians 12:8–10; 1 Corinthians 12:28; Ephesians 4:11–12; and 1 Peter 4:9–11.

4. If you have ever done a study on spiritual gifts or taken a spiritual gifts test, what have you determined are your gifts? How are you using them now? If you do not know what your gifts are, name one from the verses above that you feel like you may have.

5. Of the five excuses that Moses gives the Lord, which one are you most likely to use as your own excuse:

"Who am I?"   *Your self-esteem*
"Suppose . . ."   *Your fears*
"What if . . ."   *Your future*

"I have never been . . ."   *Your past*
"Please send someone else."   *Your reluctance*

6. Read the parable of the talents in Matthew 25:14–30. What is the master's reply to the first two servants? What is his reply to the third servant? What does this passage teach you about serving God?

7. Ephesians 4:1 says, "As a prisoner for the Lord, then, I urge you to live a life worthy of the calling you have received." How is God calling you to serve Him? What are at least three practical things that you can do right now in order to obey His call?

8. *Memorize* Colossians 3:17: "And whatever you do, whether in word or deed, do it all in the name of the Lord Jesus, giving thanks to God the Father through him."

Part Three

UNSHAKABLE

Chapter 13

Before You Shake Your Tambourine

Challenge #1—Brace Yourself

By now you have seen what an impact the story of Jephthah's daughter has made in my life. I hope that in the previous chapters her story has affected you as well. But I cannot conclude this book without leaving you with a few challenges.

After studying JD's story, you've seen a picture of the type of person you want to become—a woman who is more preoccupied with who she is in God's eyes than with who she is as a single. You've taken a long journey on which you've accomplished many noteworthy things. You've redefined independence, discovered your designer genes, evaluated the grace in your life, realized the importance of your grasp of Scripture, sought God in the mountains, reached out to godly girlfriends, learned how to grieve and then get up, found inspiration for purity, and admitted the importance of serving God with your gifts.

It took an unnamed, unmarried, and unshakable girl from an obscure passage in the Old Testament, but you are finally beginning to experience peace with where God has you in life. Hopefully you're not just walking away with peace; you're walking away with inspiration also! You want to share her story with your single friends. You want to mentor those younger than you to teach them to discover who they are in Christ before marital status even becomes an issue. You want to plan a trip to the "mountains" for you and your single girlfriends so you can meet with God together and celebrate what He has taught you!

> Before you shake your tambourine in celebration, you need to remember one thing: not everyone has been on this journey with you.

Here is where the first challenge comes. Before you shake your tambourine in celebration, you need to remember one thing: not everyone has been on this journey with you.

You may be experiencing peace and contentment, but those around you may still feel the need to comment about or discourage your current status as a single. Friends may still encourage you to go out with non-Christians in an effort to avoid dateless Friday nights. Your parents may still remind you that they want to have grandchildren someday. You may still get a raised eyebrow when you ask for a table for one. And your grandmother may still have the audacity to ask you what's wrong with you that you're not married yet.

Before you shake your tambourine, you need to brace your-self for those kinds of comments. If you've heard them before, chances are you will continue to hear them. Remember when we talked about our words being full of grace? Not everyone has learned that lesson, and when it comes to being single, people can say some pretty rude things. Unfortunately, those words, even words used in jest, have the potential to wound us if we're not careful.

I surveyed many single women and asked them to share some comments others have made to them about their singleness. Some of them were so inappropriate that I can't even include them in this book. But others simply lacked tact, and it made me realize that I was not the only one trying to fend off un-wanted commentaries. Read some of the comments that women like you have received. (*Names have been changed to protect the innocent.*)

- **Katy, age 32:** At my little cousin's wedding (she was eigh-teen), I was the maid of honor. My brother-in-law spent the entire weekend referring to me as the "Old Maid of Honor."
- **Monica, age 34:** "So your brother and sister are getting married, and they are both younger than you? Does this upset you at all?"
- **Libby, age 27:** My grandmother to her friend: "These are my granddaughters, Ally, Christine, and Jennifer. And this is Libby, and *she's not married*" (said with a whisper, of course).
- **Tara, age 30:** At wedding showers: "So when will we be do-ing this for you?"

- **Missy, age 32:** "Why in the world would you buy a house? Don't you want to experience that first with your husband?"
- **Shelly, age 24:** At younger sister's rehearsal dinner: "So, do you think your father will do the old wedding-day switcheroo like Laban did with Rachel and Leah in the Bible?"
- **Renee, age 35:** "People shouldn't wait to have children until they're in their thirties."
- **Dawn, age 28:** From my father: "There are four million people in that town; why can't you find at least one of them to date you?"
- **Sophie, age 31:** "So how's your boyfriend? Oh, that's right; you don't have one."
- **Tina, age 39:** "There must be something seriously wrong with your future husband if it's taking the Lord this long to fix him!"

Facing Persecution

You could probably add your own comments to this list above. You've endured the parental pressures, the meddling matchmakers, and the rude remarks yourself. Do they still offend you, or do you find humor in them?

It took me a long time before I could move from being offended to being entertained. When I told one of my grandmothers that I wanted her to be escorted down the aisle and seated at a place of honor in my future wedding, she laughed and said, "Well, I'm not going to live *that* long, you know!" Her words lingered in my mind for a long time, and I felt my peace begin to waiver.

Some time later, my other grandmother blurted out in the middle of a family dinner, "I know, Emily. Maybe you could look into one of those Rent-a-Husband programs!" This time I didn't find the remark offensive; I found it hilarious! The comments were equally inappropriate and equally hurtful, yet my response to them was different. What changed?

What changed for me is that I came to realize that such comments are actually a form of persecution. I don't mean to over-dramatize it, but whenever you are being harassed on the basis of your belief in God (specifically, in your belief that God has a plan and a time frame for your love life), that's persecution.

Now I know that my sweet little grandmas are not consciously out to persecute me, but they came from an age when women married right out of high school and had children who were in junior high by the time they were my age. It is hard for them to see my life as normal and acceptable because it is so different from what was normal and acceptable back in their days.

> When you become vocal about your belief that God's ways are higher than your ways, others may attempt to belittle your faith.

Likewise, those who married their high school sweethearts can't imagine the desire to try out Internet dating via Christian Web sites. And those who had three children by their twenty-fifth birthdays cannot fathom having children in their late thirties.

When you become vocal about your belief that God's ways are higher than your ways, others may attempt to belittle your faith. It may come in the form of teasing, harassment, or even full-blown persecution. "Dear friends, do not be surprised at the painful trial you are suffering, as though something strange were happening to you. But rejoice that you participate in the sufferings of Christ, so that you may be overjoyed when his glory is revealed" (1 Peter 4:12–13).

Persecution is a promise for the believer. You may be ridiculed for your belief in creation versus evolution, or you may be rejected for turning down drugs or alcohol. Thankfully, most of us will never have to endure persecution that is so intense it demands our lives. However, in some way, even if it's when we're teased because of our faith in God's plan for our love lives, we endure our own form of persecution. "In fact, everyone who wants to live a godly life in Christ Jesus will be persecuted" (2 Timothy 3:12).

Persecution is also a blessing for believers. Matthew 5:10 says, "Blessed are those who are persecuted because of righteousness, for theirs is the kingdom of heaven." Are you trying, despite worldly pressures, to be holy in your dating life (or your nondating life)? God will bless you for your righteousness.

Responding to Persecution

I'm not going to pretend that the comments don't hurt sometimes. But when you linger on the insults and doubts of others, you are giving more weight to their opinions than you are to God's promises. God promises to take care of you. He promises that His ways are higher than your ways. "No good thing does he withhold from those whose walk is blameless" (Psalm 84:11). Though others may imply that God is "withholding" a husband from you, that is simply not the case. His plans are perfect, and He wants to wow you with what He has in store for you.

I love the words of Ephesians 3:20. "Now to him who is able to do immeasurably more than all we ask or imagine, according to his power that is at work within us, to him be glory in the church and in Christ Jesus throughout all generations, for ever and ever! Amen."

Whatever fairy tale you have imagined for your life, God can do immeasurably more! Don't be so quick to give up on Him. He longs to give you the fairy tale He's planned for you because He loves you and because He wants to be glorified through it.

That being said, what do we do when everyone from our co-workers to our family members constantly offers advice, comments, and insults without merit? Jesus says we should pray for them. "But I tell you: Love your enemies and pray for those who persecute you" (Matthew 5:44).

Your actions during your time as a single will speak volumes to those around you. Your coworkers will find your faith odd, and they may become curious about the source of your strength. Your family members will be humbled by your peace with God's timing. Pray that your attitude and actions become a witness to those around you.

Challenge #2—Pass It On

When I surveyed the single women around me, I got so much more than a list of humorous, yet stinging, comments. I also got a glimpse into the hearts of other singles. From many, I saw evidence of wisdom and faith that was so unwavering, it made me consider handing them my outline and having them write this book.

I could see that others had been on their own journey with

God already. They admitted having the fears, the doubts, and the uncertainties that I experienced, but God, in His awesome faithfulness, had already pulled them through it.

But I could see shades of hopelessness appearing in others' answers. It broke my heart to read comments like, "I keep wondering if something is wrong with me." I wanted to shout back at the paper, "Nothing is wrong with you! God made you! He loves you!"

Another woman was sick of hearing, "God's timing is perfect." "Duh, I know that," she wrote. "But it doesn't take away the anguish of longing to be loved and still not being loved at the age of 39 while everyone around me seems to find that." I wanted to encourage her as well. "It's okay to feel that way. Grieve your singleness! God understands, and He wants to comfort you in ways that only He can."

Another girl wrote, "Most days, I don't mind being single. Other days, it's the worst thing ever, and I just wish that God would hurry it up."

You can probably relate to her honesty. Some days you love the freedom, the fun, and the excitement that being single has to offer. You can come and go as you please. You can spend your money as you please, and you can eat cereal and green beans for dinner if you want.

But other days you crawl into bed and long for someone to be there beside you. You see a little girl holding her mommy's hand, and you ache to have your own children.

Before you shake your tambourine, before you check off the lessons in this book as "done," I want you to remember that the good days come and go. And this is where we can help each other.

You may be in the middle of a time of peace and joy after reading this book and spending time with God in the mountains. But someone else around you might still be in the middle of the valley. Open your heart to that person. Pray that God would make you sensitive to the woman who is struggling and allow you an opportunity to minister to her.

We need our girls. We need to know that we're not alone in our struggles. I challenge every single one of you to either pass this book to a friend when you're done or else buy your friend her own copy.

But don't just hand it to her with a pious, "I thought this book could help you" attitude. Tell her how you've struggled. Tell her how you're *still* struggling. Share with her specifically what God is teaching you, and give it to her with the promise of praying with her and chatting with her over coffee at a future date.

Challenge #3—Keep It Going

The last thing I want to leave with you is the reminder that this book encompasses encouragement and principles that will continue to benefit you in the next chapter of your life (whatever that chapter may be). Before you shake your tambourine, before you write this book off as something that might benefit you as a single and nothing else, I want you to remember that.

A recurring theme in the surveys I received was that women were tired of tips and opinions about dating and not dating. They didn't want to hear anything else about "how to get a man to marry you" or "how to prepare for marriage." Instead, they longed for something they could relate to as singles but that kept the primary focus on their relationship with God.

I hope the story of Jephthah's daughter filled the void that you all felt. While we can relate to her because she is single, we can continue to benefit from her examples because they apply to all of us, regardless of our marital status.

Don't forget about this exceptional girl when and if you become a wife.

Marriage may be around the corner for some of you. If so, it would be wise to take the lessons learned about words of grace with you into your marriage. Perhaps your future father-in-law is not the man of God that you had hoped for. It would be great to remember the Father who sits on a throne and not on a pedestal.

As a new mom, you'll long to meet other new moms, and you'll be reminded of the importance of having girlfriends in your similar walk of life. And if infertility, unemployment, or any other difficult circumstance is in your future, you'll be an encouragement to others when you practice nonalcoholic grief.

In the final chapter, you will find a review of everything you have learned through the life of this unnamed, unmarried, and unshakable scriptural heroine. Just as the young women of Israel set aside a specific time each year to commemorate the life of Jephthah's daughter, I urge you to do the same by regularly participating in the Tambourine Tribute. It is a refresher course that compiles some of the key points of each chapter with fresh questions to consider as you evaluate the presence of each godly principle we learned about in the previous chapters.

Don't forget about this exceptional girl when and if you become a wife. Remember, she is not just another godly woman who taught us how to live better as singles. Rather, she is a single woman who taught us, by example, how to be godly.

I pray that you have been blessed by this remarkable young woman, just as I have been. I hope her story has been a comfort to you as a single, and I pray that God will use her story to bless you again in your future.

I don't know your name, but I pray that God will bless you. I don't know your abilities, but I pray that God will use you. And I don't know what the future holds for you, but I pray that you would remain unshakable!

Chapter 14

The Tambourine Tribute

From this comes the Israelite custom that each year the young women of Israel go out for four days to commemorate the daughter of Jephthah the Gileadite (Judges 11:39–40).

How the Tribute Works

Just as the young women of Israel set aside four days a year to commemorate the obedient life of Jephthah's daughter, the Tambourine Tribute serves as a catalyst for you to do the same. But don't think of this opportunity as the chance to honor her so much as the chance to honor her God for what He taught you *through* her.

The chapter is broken down into ten sections, corresponding to the ten chapters in part 2. Each section opens with a piece of JD's story, and then provides several *Points to Ponder* that you will recognize from the previous chapters. The *Questions to Consider* are new and fresh, so they will stir your heart no matter what chapter of life you are in when you read them. Finally, the *Message to Memorize* will review the memory verses suggested throughout the book.

You don't have to set aside four days for the Tambourine Tribute. You can set aside a long weekend, a week, or even a ten-day stretch if you like. If a particular section convicts you more than others, put the tribute on pause so you can go back and read the corresponding chapter, research the subject in your Bible, or spend extra time in prayer.

The Tambourine Tribute is not to be read quickly in one setting. It is to be read slowly, prayerfully, and regularly.

Before You Begin

- Read the story of Jephthah's daughter (Judges 11:34–40) in several different translations. (You can go to www.bible-gateway.com to access the Bible in many different translations.)
- Have a notebook with you so you can journal your thoughts to God as He prompts you.
- Pray specifically that God will speak to you during this time.

YOUR GUMPTION

Verse to Reference

When Jephthah returned to his home in Mizpah, who should come out to meet him but his daughter, dancing to the sound of tambourines! (Judges 11:34).

Points to Ponder

- Gumption is discovering that your identity has nothing to do with who you are and everything to do with who God is.
- Gumption is understanding that waiting on God is an active task, not a passive one.
- Gumption is not becoming an independent woman but becoming a woman solely dependent on Christ.

Questions to Consider

- What has God taught you recently about who He is?
- What, specifically, are you waiting for God to do in your life?
- How are you waiting on Him (serving Him) in the meantime?
- Have you become more or less dependent on God in the past year?

Message to Memorize

For you created my inmost being; you knit me together in my mother's womb. I praise you because I am fearfully and wonderfully made (Psalm 139:13–14).

YOUR GENES

Verse to Reference

She was an only child. Except for her he had neither son nor daughter (Judges 11:34).

Points to Ponder

- You have a Father who sits not on a pedestal but on a throne.
- Through Christ, you are a child of God.
- God's children receive an inheritance only God's Son could orchestrate—the inheritance of eternal life.
- Knowing your Father means knowing the promises He offers His children.

Questions to Consider

- How is your relationship with your father, if he is still alive?
- How is your relationship with your heavenly Father?
- What is a promise of God that you have claimed as your own recently?

Message to Memorize

How great is the love the Father has lavished on us, that we should be called children of God! And that is what we are! (1 John 3:1).

YOUR GRACE

Verse to Reference

When he saw her, he tore his clothes and cried, "Oh! My daughter! You have made me miserable and wretched, because I have made a vow to the LORD that I cannot break." "My father," she replied (Judges 11:35–36).

Points to Ponder

- Grace is giving someone something that is undeserved.
- Grace does not come naturally; it comes *super*naturally.
- God's grace is the funnel through which all of His blessings flow.
- God's grace is sufficient.
- When you extend grace to others in the things you say to them, you mirror the grace that God has extended to you.

Questions to Consider

- How have you shown grace to someone recently?
- What was the last thing you received that you really didn't deserve?
- How has God's grace helped you endure suffering?
- What words have you said lately that have not been full of grace?

Message to Memorize

God made him who had no sin to be sin for us, so that in him we might become the righteousness of God (2 Corinthians 5:21).

YOUR GRASP

Verse to Reference

"You have given your word to the LORD. Do to me just as you promised, now that the LORD has avenged you of your enemies, the Ammonites" (Judges 11:36).

Points to Ponder

- The Bible is a love letter from God's heart to yours.
- If you want to know God and His will for your life, you must strengthen your grasp of Scripture.
- For the growing Christian, Scripture memory is not an option. It is a command.
- Scripture memory transforms your thinking into His thinking when it's His words that are echoing in your mind and not your own.
- He gave you the Bible in order that through it, you may see Him. It's a book where the lost get found, the blind can see, good triumphs over evil, and everyone gets a second chance.

Questions to Consider

- How often have you been reading your Bible?
- What distractions have kept you from reading your Bible more?
- What has God's Word taught you lately?
- What verse has meant the most to you recently?
- What Scriptures have you memorized in the last year?

Message to Memorize

I have hidden your word in my heart that I might not sin against you (Psalm 119:11).

YOUR GOD

Verse to Reference

"But grant me this one request," she said. "Give me two months to roam the hills and weep with my friends, because I will never marry." "You may go," he said. And he let her go for two months (Judges 11:37–38).

Points to Ponder

- In order to make the most of your mountain moments, you must realize that proximity to people is not the issue. The issue is your proximity to God.
- Having a true mountaintop experience does not involve your being alone with your thoughts; it involves your being alone with God's thoughts.
- Though God is the same yesterday, today, and forever, He is so big and so multifaceted that He can appear to us new every morning.
- On the mountain of the Lord, it will be provided.
- God sees eternity when all we see is today.

Questions to Consider

- Where is your "mountain" (the place where you go to meet with God)?
- How often do you go to your mountain?
- What are you praising God for today?
- How has God provided for you?
- What has God shown you from His perspective that you have been unable to see from your own perspective?

Message to Memorize

Send forth your light and your truth, let them guide me; let them bring me to your holy mountain, to the place where you dwell (Psalm 43:3).

YOUR GIRLS

Verse to Reference

She and the girls went into the hills (Judges 11:38).

Points to Ponder

- Friendship involves being "one in spirit" with another person.
- Add to your circle of friends with women who are in your similar stage of life.
- Help your friends in actions, not just with words.
- Anyone can tell you what you want to hear, but it takes a true friend to tell you the truth, even when the truth will hurt.
- Jealousy has no place among friends.

Questions to Consider

- What is your current stage of life?
- Do you have friends who are also in that stage?
- How have you helped your friends in your actions?
- Have you been rebuked by a friend recently?
- What do your friends have that you don't have?
- Are you genuinely happy for their successes?

Message to Memorize

A friend loves at all times, and a brother is born for adversity (Proverbs 17:17).

YOUR GRIEF

Verse to Reference

. . . and wept because she would never marry (Judges 11:38).

Points to Ponder

- Tears have a place in your Christian walk. Grief is allowed. Sorrow is acceptable.
- Jesus wept.
- Sometimes you are not pouring out grief, but whine.
- Happiness pouts when it doesn't understand God's ways. Joy places God's sovereignty above His mystery.
- If you want your grief to turn to joy, shift your attention away from yourself and focus on God.

Questions to Consider

- What situation are you grieving over now?
- Have you poured your heart out to God?
- Do you ever find yourself whining about your circumstances?
- How have you shifted your attention away from yourself and focused on God?

Message to Memorize

Weeping may remain for a night, but rejoicing comes in the morning (Psalm 30:5).

YOUR GUARANTEE

Verse to Reference

After the two months, she returned to her father and he did to her as he had vowed (Judges 11:39).

Points to Ponder

- God's ways cannot be summed up in a nice, neat little formula. His plans are too creative to be that predictable.
- It is not necessarily important *how* you move beyond your grief, but *that* you move beyond it.
- God never promises that all things are good. He simply promises that He can use all things for good.
- You can find purpose in your tears by knowing that you will be able to be a blessing to someone else who goes through a situation similar to yours.

Questions to Consider

- How has God surprised you with His blessings lately?
- What are some bad things that God has used for good in your life?
- Are you still grieving, or have you turned your grief into action?
- How have you comforted someone else in the past year?

Message to Memorize

"For my thoughts are not your thoughts, neither are your ways my ways," declares the Lord. "As the heavens are higher than the earth, so are my ways higher than your ways and my thoughts than your thoughts" (Isaiah 55:8–9).

YOUR GUILTLESSNESS

Verse to Reference

And she was a virgin (Judges 11:39).

Points to Ponder

- When it comes to sex, Satan has a whole arsenal of weapons that he can use against you.
- Guiltlessness is not merely an absence of fornication; rather, it is the presence of purity.
- Guiltlessness begins in your mind.

Questions to Consider

- How are you being tempted with sexual sins?
- Is there a particular person or situation that is tempting you more than others?
- What would God say about your thought life?
- How are you striving for purity in the things you watch, do, and say?

Message to Memorize

But just as he who called you is holy, so be holy in all you do; for it is written: "Be holy, because I am holy" (1 Peter 1:15–16).

YOUR GUIDANCE

Verse to Reference

From this comes the Israelite custom that each year the young women of Israel go out for four days to commemorate the daughter of Jephthah the Gileadite (Judges 11:39–40).

Points to Ponder

- It's easy to shy away from leadership when you're going through the valley.
- God does not want anything from you—your service, your money, your talents, or anything else—until He has *you* first.
- God wants to use you now, and He's waiting to hear you say, "Here I am."
- Spiritual gifts are not meant to limit the ways and opportunities for you to serve God.
- God can still use you in spite of who you are.

Questions to Consider

- Does God have your heart?
- Are you available for Him to use?
- What is keeping you from serving in your local church?
- What sounds scarier to you right now—to be used by God, or to not be used by God?
- What is God calling you to do for Him?

Message to Memorize

And whatever you do, whether in word or deed, do it all in the name of the Lord Jesus, giving thanks to God the Father through him (Colossians 3:17).

Note to the Reader

The publisher invites you to share your response to the message of this book by writing Discovery House Publishers, P.O. Box 3566, Grand Rapids, MI 49501, U.S.A. For information about other Discovery House books, music, videos, or DVDs, contact us at the same address or call 1-800-653-8333. Find us on the Internet at http://www.dhp.org/ or send e-mail to books@dhp.org.